Blessed John Henry Newman

A Richly Illustrated Portrait

Blessed John Henry Newman

A Richly Illustrated Portrait

Sister Kathleen Dietz FSO
Sister Mary-Birgit Dechant FSO
Editors

International Centre Of Newman Friends
The Spiritual Family The Work

Foreword by Father Ian Ker

Freedom Publishing
AUSTRALIA

Gracewing

First published in 2010

Gracewing
2 Southern Avenue, Leominster
Herefordshire HR6 0QF
United Kingdom

ISBN 978 085244 724 6
Published in Australia
by
Freedom Publishing Pty Ltd
35 Whitehorse Road
Balwyn
Victoria 3103

Illustrations courtesy
of Michael Pitt-Payne

Additional typesetting by Action Publishing Technology,
Gloucester GL1 1SP

Printed in Italy
by Grafiche Flaminia

Contents

Foreword 1

Introduction 3

1. The Beginnings 7

2. Newman at Oxford: The Trinity Years 19

3. Newman at Oxford: The Oriel Years 29

4. The College and the Convert 57

5. The Oratorian Years 79

6. The Cardinal 111

Epilogue: The College after Newman 139

List of Illustrations 141

Abbreviations 148

Bibliography 149

Acknowledgements 151

Dedication

This book is dedicated to all
who have contributed to the building up
of the permanent exhibition
and of the specialized library
at The College in Littlemore, Oxford

Foreword

Sisters Kathleen Dietz and Mary-Birgit Dechant of the Spiritual Family the Work are to be congratulated on producing such a beautiful portrait of John Henry Newman, whom Pope Benedict XVI will beatify this September. It is beautiful both in the simplicity of the text and in the accompanying pictures.

This illustrated life of Newman is an excellent introduction for those who know little or nothing of the great cardinal. But Newman scholars, too, will be delighted by the illustrations that bring to life the man and his times. These illustrations are the result of a good deal of hard work. When the Sisters of the Spiritual Family the Work underook the care of the College at Littlemore in 1987, they found a small number of pictures and memorabilia. This collection has grown substantially over the years since. Much of this was due to the enthusiasm of Sister Brigitte Maria Hoegemann, who was the first superior of the Sisters' community of The Work at Littlemore.

There are many people, not scholars or intellectuals, who would like to be introduced to the man soon to be beatified. The miraculous cure that has enabled Newman to be beatified was of an American, Jack Sullivan, suddenly afflicted by a severe spinal disease, who knew next to nothing about Newman when he urgently sought his intercession so that he might complete his studies for the married diaconate. It was not, therefore, an academic who had studied Newman's thought and writings who prayed to Newman and was healed, but somebody who describes himself as a very ordinary person. And so those of us who pray for Newman's canonisation and very confidently hope that he will be declared a Doctor of the Church, must wish that many more people will seek his intercession. I am confident that this richly illustrated portrait will draw many to the holiness of Newman so that they turn to him in their needs.

Ian Ker

Introduction

When Sisters of The Spiritual Family The Work arrived at The College at Littlemore in 1986, they found a modest number of Newman pictures and memorabilia. Over the years, especially through the expertise, enthusiasm and perseverance of Sr Brigitte Maria Hoegemann FSO, this has been built up into a substantial collection which is displayed on the walls and in the showcases of what used to be Newman's library. The Sisters use this exhibition to present Newman to those who tour The College. This book makes the collection available to a wider audience for the first time and in timely fashion, given Newman's beatification on 19 September 2010. We have selected quotations fitting with the photographs of the collection so that the reader enjoys the double effect of picture and word; walking with Newman, as it were, through the collection.

The presentation of the book is chronological, making it easy for the reader to follow the line of Bl. John Henry Newman's life, and the quotations selected to go with the photographs show the various sides or aspects of Newman within this chronological framework, such that by the end of the book, a clear outline of the whole man will be imprinted in the mind and heart of the reader.

John Henry Newman has been misunderstood and misrepresented since he first became a public figure in his own lifetime. A man at once intellectually brilliant and keenly sensitive, relentlessly practical and marvellously alive to the wonders of everyday life, he was far from being the hyper-sensitive, melancholic recluse painted by his first biographer, Wilfred Ward. By nature solitary, he nonetheless had many and deep friendships, and kept up a prodigious correspondence with friends and acquaintances. He was a man very aware of the signs of his times, and perceptive in understanding how to answer them. A leader, but not a dominator, he was never really aware of the influence he had in Oxford. Though generally gentle and kind in his dealings with friends and acquaintances, he surprised some with his intractability and tenacity in the face of opposition, and his uncompromising adherence to principle. What held all these different aspects and traits together in harmony was Newman's great love for Christ and his faith in God's loving providence.

With his beatification, numbers are being added to the many people who have a liking for or an interest in Newman, but who have at the same time only a vague notion about him as a person. Most are not inclined, nor do they have the time, to read a full biography of him. It is hoped that this book will fill a gap in Newman literature by presenting Newman for just such people, as well as for the veteran Newman lover. As far as possible, we have let Newman tell his story in his own words so that the texts reflect in themselves something of Newman's character, and the reader gets a fair sampling of the charm and beauty of Newman's writings.

Many people will perhaps wonder why Newman was beatified, what made him holy. This book seeks to indicate the answer. His was not a life of extraordinary signs and wonders, of visions and ecstasies, or of great physical trials. His holiness, as the holiness of all God's Saints, consisted in living the virtues of faith, hope and charity, in accepting and obeying God's will in the ordinary, everyday circumstances of life, as well as in the extraordinary trials with which his life was filled. His was in fact a heroic life lived to the full for Christ and his Church.

The Beginnings

Chapter 1

The Beginnings

(1801-1817)

JOHN HENRY NEWMAN was born 21 February 1801 in the City of London, not far from the site of the present London Stock Exchange. He was the eldest of the six children born to John and Jemima (Fourdrinier) Newman. His father was a banker and partner in the bank of Ramsbottom, Newman and Ramsbottom. He had a happy childhood and the comfort of a loving, close-knit family.

When he was seven years old, John's father sent him to Ealing School where he excelled to such an extent that the headmaster, Dr Nicholas, used to say that no other boy passed more quickly through the school, from the bottom to the top, than John Henry Newman. He was an affectionate, but quick-tempered boy, studious and, though not given to games with the other boys, nonetheless full of fun. His recreation consisted in reading and writing. No loner, he was the ringleader of the secret club of senior boys called the Spy Club, whose members wrote the periodical called "The Portfolio". Newman himself wrote two periodicals, or papers, as he called them, called "Spy" and "Anti-Spy", written, as their names imply, against each other, as well as a later one called "The Beholder". He loved acting and even wrote a burlesque opera when he was fourteen, composing tunes for the songs.

In March 1816 his father's bank had to close. The partners managed to pay everyone off, but they could not keep the bank open. The family house had to be let and Mr Newman had to try his hand at managing a brewery in Alton, Hampshire, a position he got through his partners' connections. John Henry remained at Ealing through the summer holidays and the autumn term of 1816 was his last at the school. That autumn term was to prove a pivotal point of his life.

The Newman family was an ordinary Church of England family, as far as religion and faith are concerned. They were Bible Christians and their religion consisted mainly in reading the Bible or having it read. John Henry had, as he himself put it, no formed religious convictions as a boy, until that autumn term when, between August and December 1816, he went through what he would later term his "first conversion".

"When I was fifteen," Newman was to write nearly 50 years later in his *Apologia*, "in the autumn of 1816, a great change of thought took place in me and I fell under the influence of a definite creed …" (*Apo.*, 4).

His conversion began, as did subsequent great moments in his life, with illness. In this illness he felt "the heavy hand of God" and he could never speak about "the experiences before and after" except to say that they were "awful, and known only to God" (*AW*, 268). Nonetheless, the illness opened his mind and heart, and made him docile to the guiding hand of the classics master, Rev. Walter Mayers, a fervent and pious evangelical minister, who was the human instrument of the "beginning of divine faith" in Newman. Mayers gave Newman several books to read, all Calvinistic in character among them a work of Thomas Scott, whom Newman came to admire and revere so much that he thought of paying a visit to his parsonage so that he could meet the man to whom he, humanly speaking, almost owed his soul (cf. *Apo.*, 5).

He also read Milner's *Church History* and encountered the Fathers of the Church for the first time in it. At the same time he read Newton's book on the prophecies about the Antichrist. The conflicting ideas gained from the two books, love of the Fathers and the early Church, and the conviction that the Pope was the Antichrist predicted by Daniel, St. Paul and St. John, had a crippling effect on his intellect and made him inconsistent in his thinking for many years, as he himself attests (cf. *Apo.*, 6).

But the lasting and over-riding effect of his conversion was the understanding that there is an objective truth independent of our thoughts and feelings, independent of us. This dogmatic principle became the foundation for all his subsequent thinking and acting. It therefore provides the key to understanding Newman and his writings correctly.

Plaque on the London Stock Exchange indicating the place of Newman's birth

Saturday 21 February 1801 *I was born*

Thursday 9 April *baptised*

LD I, 3.

The Fourdrinier Family. Newman's mother is next to her father, who has his arm around her

When he was quite young, John Henry once had a struggle of wills with his mother and lost: "You see, John," his mother said, "you did not get your own way." "No," said John, "but I tried very hard!"

M. Trevor, The Pillar of the Cloud, 9.

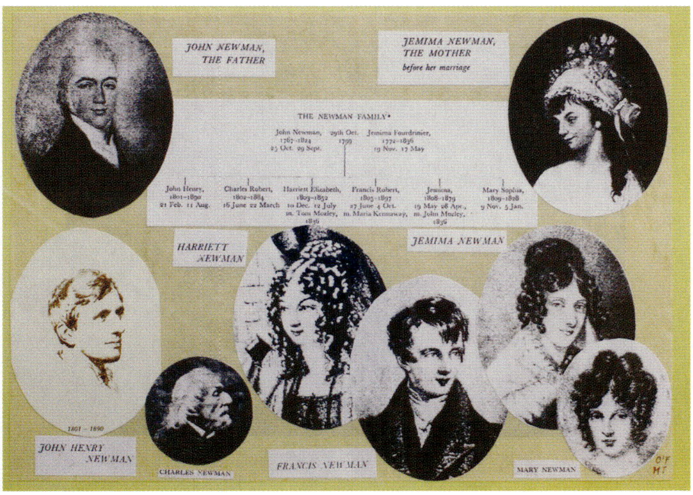

Collage of the Newman Family
– from top left, John and Jemima (Fourdrinier) Newman, parents,
John, Charles, Harriett, Francis, Jemima, Mary

We have not had to weep over the death of those we love. We are not disunited by internal variance – we are not parted from each other by circumstances we cannot control. We have kind and indulgent parents, and our tastes, dispositions, and pursuits are the same. How grateful ought we to be! Surely it is a joyful thing that that distress which must be leaves unimpaired, or rather heightened, all domestic affection and love.

LD I, 113, Letter to Mrs Newman, 26 October 1821.

Greycourt House at Ham, Richmond, the Newman family's country retreat until September 1807

I have been looking at the windows of our house at Ham near Richmond, where I lay aged five looking at the candles stuck in them in celebration of the victory of Trafalgar. ... I know more about it than any house I have been in since, and could pass an examination in it.

LD XX, 23, Letter to Miss Holmes, 5 August 1861.

My home is now a thousand miles away;
Yet in my thoughts its every image fair
Rises as keen, as I still linger'd there,
And, turning me, could all I loved survey. ...

VV, 85, Memory.

The joyful 21 again approaches when our books are closed according to delightful custom, and when I hope for the additional pleasure of seeing you all well and happy at home. Already in imagination I pay my respects to the mince Pies, Turkies, and the other good things of Christmas. In the mean time the Notches on my wooden Calendar diminish apace....

LD I, 9-10, Letter to Elizabeth Newman, 6 December 1811.

17 Southampton St (now Southampton Place), London, where the Newman family lived 1802 to 1816, and 1819 to 1821

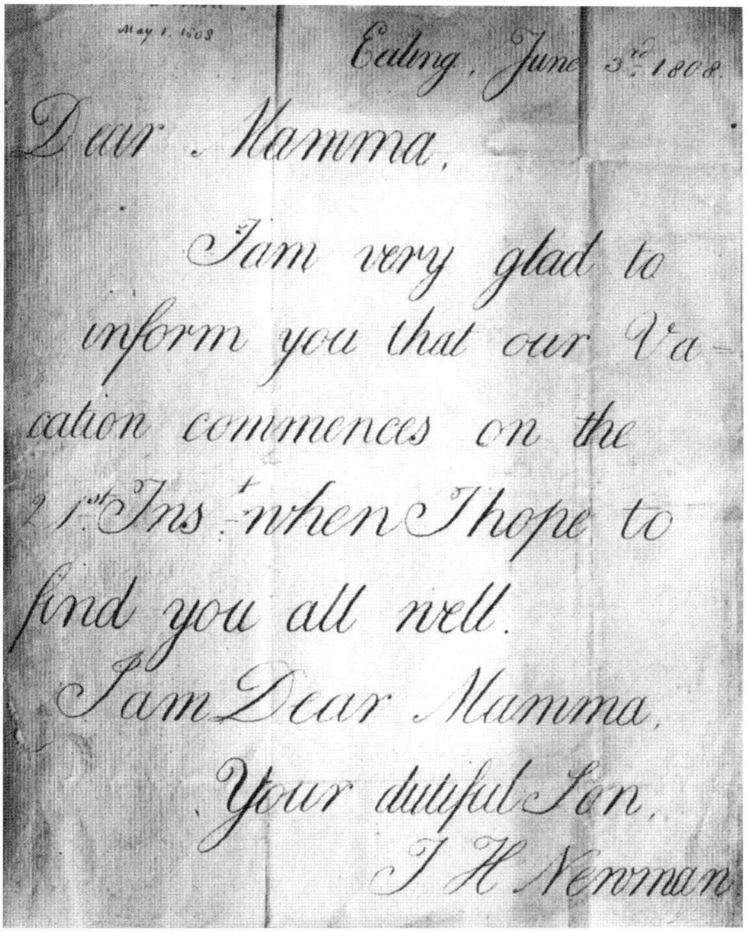

May 1. 1808

Ealing, June 3rd 1808.

Dear Mamma,

I am very glad to inform you that our Vacation commences on the 21st Inst. when I hope to find you all well.

I am Dear Mamma,

Your dutiful Son,

J H Newman

Newman's first letter home – June 3, 1808, sent from Ealing School, which he attended from 1808 to 1816

Dear Mamma,

I am very glad to inform you that our Vacation commences on the 21st Inst. when I hope to find you all well.

I am Dear Mamma,

Your dutiful Son,

J H Newman.

LDI, 4.

Great Ealing School, where Newman had his "first conversion" in the autumn of 1816

When I was fourteen, I read Paine's Tracts against the Old Testament, and found pleasure in thinking of the objections which were contained in them. ... Also, I recollect copying out some French verses, perhaps Voltaire's, in denial of the immortality of the soul, and saying to myself something like "How dreadful, but how plausible!" When I was fifteen, (in the autumn of 1816) a great change of thought took place in me. I fell under the influences of a definite Creed, and received into my intellect impressions of dogma, which, through God's mercy, have never been effaced or obscured.

Apo., 3-4.

The Church of St. Mary, Ealing, as it was during Newman's time at Ealing School

I was brought up from a child to take great delight in reading the Bible; but I had no formed religious convictions till I was fifteen. Of course I had a perfect knowledge of my Catechism.

Apo., 1.

The writer who made a deeper impression on my mind than any other, and to whom (humanly speaking) I almost owe my soul, Thomas Scott of Aston Sandford (Apo. 5)

What, I suppose, will strike any reader of Scott's history and writings, is his bold unworldliness and vigorous independence of mind. He followed truth wherever it led him .... It was he who first planted deep in my mind the fundamental Truth of religion. ... I deeply felt his influence; and for years I used almost as proverbs what I considered to be the scope and issue of his doctrine, 'Holiness before peace,' and 'Growth the only evidence of life.'

Apo., 5.

Newman at Oxford

The Trinity Years

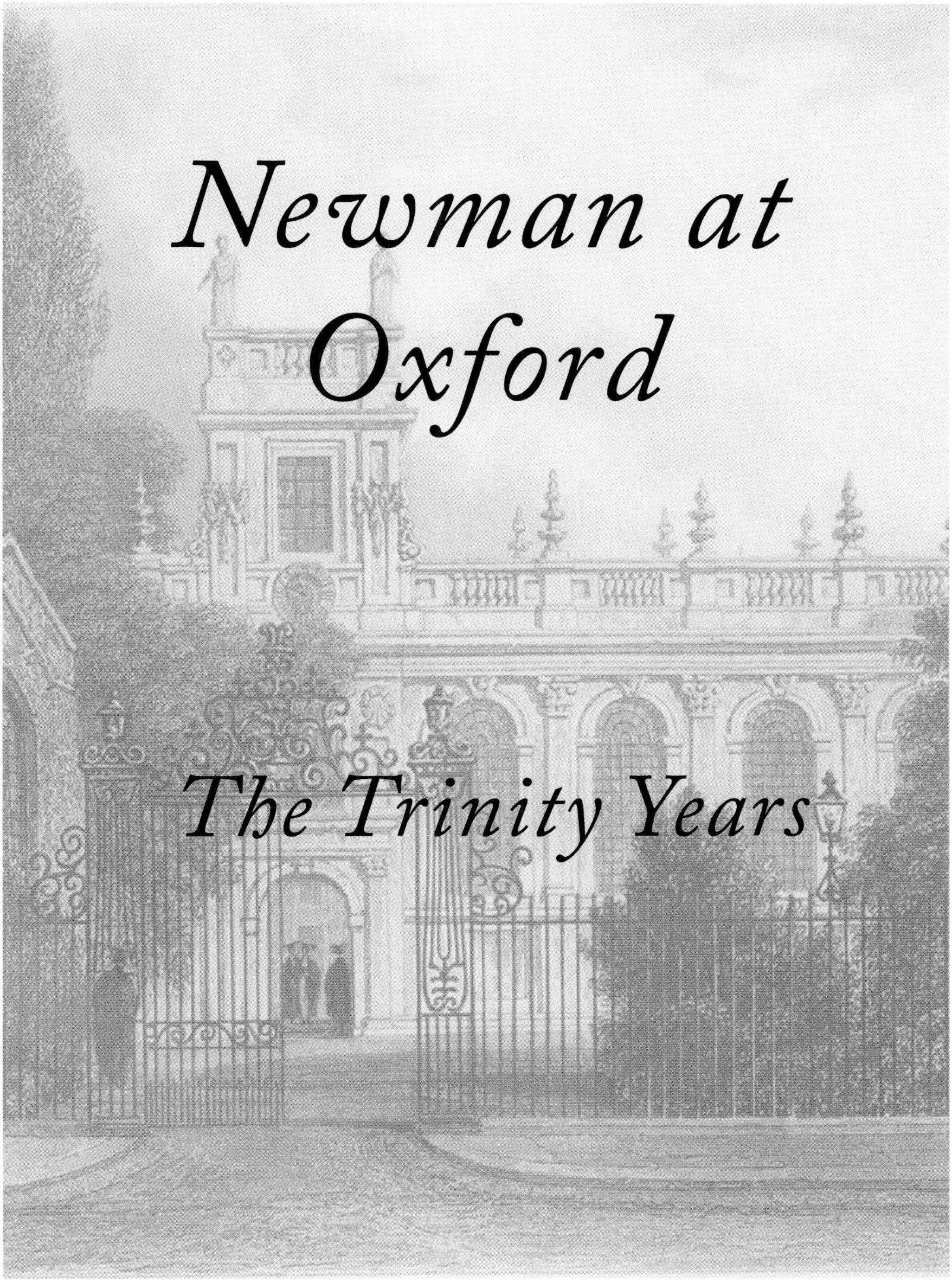

Chapter 2

Newman at Oxford

The Trinity Years
(1817-1822)

NEWMAN began his studies at Trinity College, Oxford, at the very young age of 16. College life presented a whole new world to him and he recorded it for his family with the enthusiasm and naiveté of a neophyte. After some contests of will with undergraduates of a less serious bent who were determined to make him join them in their wine parties, he settled down to serious reading with his friend, John Bowden – the two of them often reading between eleven and twelve hours a day.

Not all was study, however. Bowden and Newman dabbled in writing and publishing for a short time, and Newman continued to play his violin, for which he was known at the college. He once wrote to his sister, Harriett, that he had been invited to join an Oxford don who played bass and who loved music far too much. Due to his enthusiasm, Newman was kept playing quartets from 7 to 12:00! "Oh my poor arm and eyes and head and back," he moaned (*LD I*, 75).

In May 1818 Newman was elected a Scholar of Trinity and he records that he began to have thoughts of a secular career. He received his B.A. in December 1820, after putting in a miserable performance in the examinations and not obtaining the hoped-for honours. After taking his degree, he tutored students to earn money to help put his brother Francis through the university. In November 1821 Newman's father was declared bankrupt and Newman began to feel a growing financial responsibility for his family. In January 1822, prompted by his father to come to a decision, he chose to dedicate his life to the Church.

During his time at Trinity the effects of Newman's "first conversion" were readily evident, not so much in his refusal to participate in drinking bouts, which was a part of his nature as much as the working of grace, but in his habitual examination of his motives, in his pondering various religious questions of greater or lesser importance, in his memorizing various parts of the Bible, and in his keen examination of conscience. He strove to be docile to God's will, but he did not hesitate to question various things he read or heard in sermons, not out of impetuosity, but from an honest application of his mind. He still had his Calvinist leanings, but had developed a great devotion to the Sacrament, which he resolved to take once a fortnight during the Long Vacation of 1821.

Trinity College, view from the garden

Newman writes about his first experiences in Trinity College to his father on 11 June 1817:

At dinner I was much entertained with the novelty of the thing. Fish, flesh and fowl, beautiful salmon, haunches of mutton, lamb etc and fine, very fine (to my taste) strong beer, served up on old pewter plates, mis-shapen earthenware jugs. Tell Mama there are gooseberry, raspberry, and apricot pies. ... Tell Harriett I have seen the fat cook.

LD I, 35, Letter to Mr Newman, 11 June 1817.

John William Bowden, the first student Newman met at Trinity

He is my oldest friend: I have been most intimate with him for above 27 years. He was sent to call on me the day after I came into residence – he introduced me to College and University – he is the link between me and Oxford.

LD X, 336-337, Letter to John Keble, 14 September 1844.

Trinity College, view of the chapel from The Broad

Speaking about a photograph of Trinity Chapel which hung in his room, Newman noted on 7 Nov. 1877:

'I look at that communion table, and recollect with what feelings I went up to it in November 1817 for my first communion – how I was in mourning for the Princess Charlotte, and had silk black gloves – and the glove would not come off when I had to receive the Bread, and I had to tear it off and spoil it in my flurry ….'

Phil. N. II, 195, 197.

After recounting his refusal to participate in a wine party, Newman's mother replied:

I was fearful you would have some difficulties to encounter. I am very thankful to know that your principles are so good, that you will be able to stem the torrent of folly and impropriety. … I must echo what your Father says; Keep up your spirits – every thing will be comfortable in a little time.

LD I, 38, Letter from Mrs Newman, 19 June 1817.

Trinity College

Trinity College, view from the garden towards the president's garden

Writing in the third person, Newman later wrote about his literary ventures at Trinity:

... Mr. Newman had, in union with his friend Mr Bowden, for a few months at the end of 1818 and the beginning of 1819 been tempted to dabble in matters foreign to academical objects. They had published a Poem [St Bartholomew's Eve], their joint composition, and commenced a small periodical ... called "The Undergraduate".... *AW, 40-41.*

Trinity College, Design for the New Buildings, 1756

In May 1818 Newman won a Trinity scholarship. Before standing for it he prayed to the Lord:

O God of heaven and earth ... So let me order my spirit, that, if I get it not, I may not be disappointed, but may praise and bless Thy name, as knowing better than myself what is good for me. O Lord God of hosts, grant it not to me, if it is likely to be a snare to me, to turn me away from Thee. May I so dispose myself that I may praise Thy name, whether I receive what I pray for, or whether I receive it not. *AW, 157,158.*

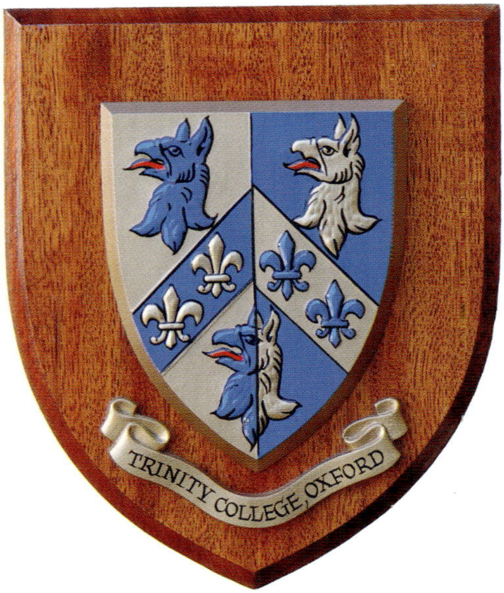

Crest of Trinity College, Oxford

Newman took his B.A. degree at Trinity College on 5 December 1820. His hopes for honours in the schools, however, were dashed.

I have cause for endless thanksgiving ... Every external advantage was in my favour. The examining Masters were kinder than it is possible for me to express; a Tutor of our College gave himself to me for the last two months to prepare me. No – it would not do. 'He hath taken away the desire of my eyes with a stroke' (Ezek 24:16). When I got into the schools I was so nervous, I could not answer half a dozen questions. The nervousness, I may add the illness, continued whenever I approached the schools, and, after a week's procrastinated efforts, I have this morning retired from the contest.

LD I, 95, Letter to an Unknown Correspondent, 1 December 1820.

His list of blessings worthily to crown
God sent his sweetest gift, sent Music down.

LD I, 'On Music – A Fragment', 39, 23–24 June 1817.

Photograph of Newman's viola with a piece of music entitled "Obiettamento" written by "the celebrated Giovanni Enrico Neandrini (Newman), Oxford 1821"

I am glad to be able to inform you and Harriett that Signor Giovanni Enrico Neandrini has finished his first Obiettamento. The melody is light and airy, and is well supported by the harmony.

LD I, 100, Letter to Mrs Newman, 28 March 1821.

Newman at Oxford

The Oriel Years

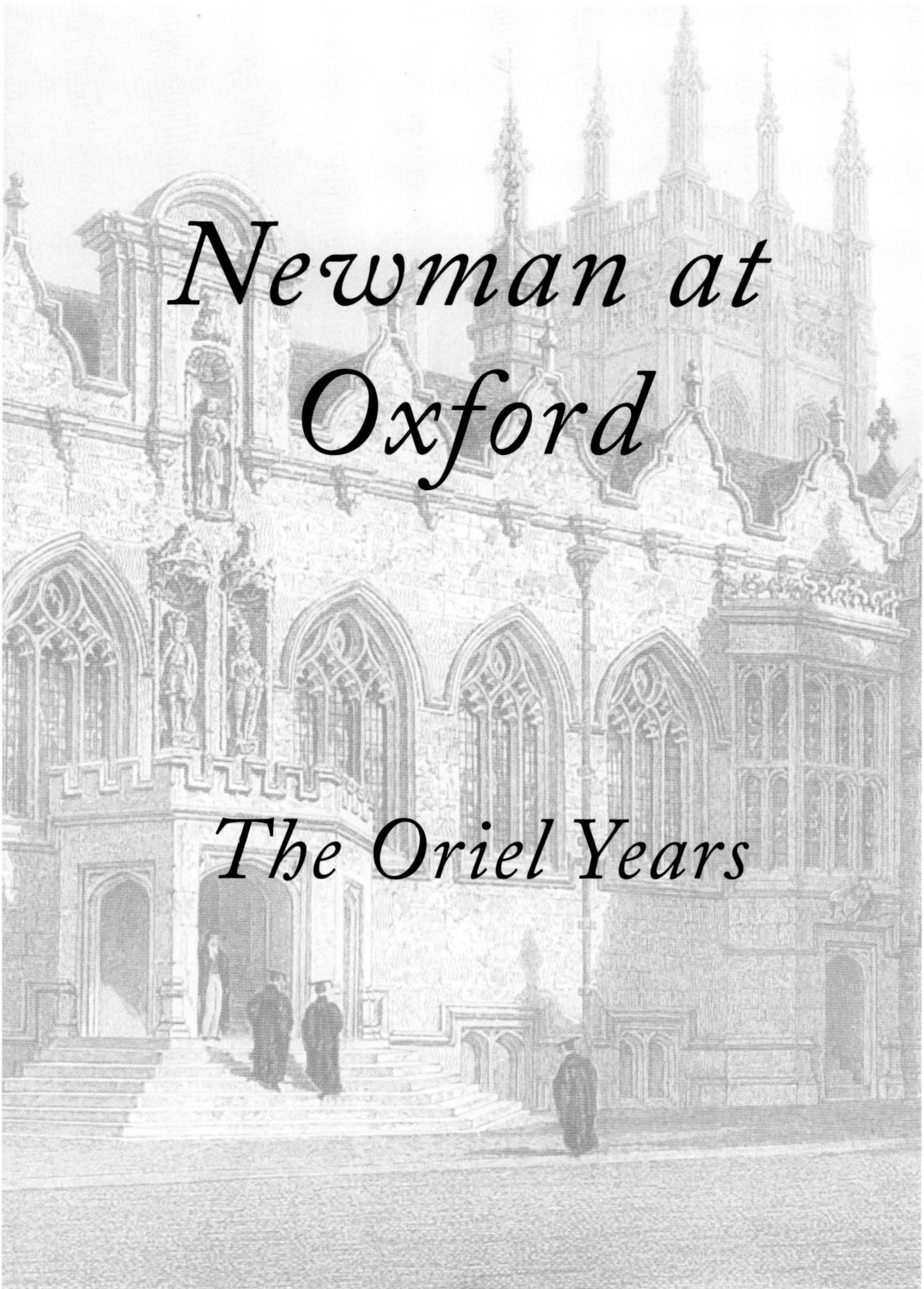

Chapter 3

Newman at Oxford

The Oriel Years

(1822-1842)

On 12 April 1822 – "of all days most memorable" – Newman was elected a Fellow of Oriel College. His chances had not been good, but a "great mercy of Divine Providence" (*AW*, 63) had overruled chance. The election secured his future, as he thought, and gave him much needed financial means which he could use to help his family, his father having become bankrupt in November of the previous year. Thus began an illustrious career at the University which lasted until 1845. Newman kept the day in reverenced memory and thanksgiving all his life.

The fellowship at Oriel meant not only money to Newman, but also a chance at an academic career, the advancement of his mind and ideas through his association with the other fellows, an environment in which he could seek the truth, and new and deep friendships. It also meant to Newman, a forum in which he could exercise his ministry, for he was ordained deacon in 1824 and Anglican priest a year later. As deacon he served as curate of St Clement, a parish just over Magdalen Bridge, not only presiding over the regular services, but also visiting all the members of the parish, as well as collecting the necessary funds for the building of a new church. He showed himself a zealous and hardworking curate, whose greatest pastoral joy was visiting the sick. It was his pastoral work at St Clement's, as much as his association with the other Oriel Fellows, which began to work in him a change in thinking, bringing him gradually to give up his Calvinistic view which made him look at people as either all good or all bad, so that, as was typical of Newman, his activity and his thinking developed together. "The whole man moves," he was to write later (*Apo.*, 169). Meanwhile, in 1825, Newman was also appointed Vice-Principal of St Alban Hall under Richard Whately, later Anglican Archbishop of Dublin.

Upon being appointed tutor at Oriel in the spring of 1826, he relinquished his curacy at St Clement's and his post at St Alban Hall, but was appointed Vicar of the University Church of St Mary the Virgin just two years later in 1828. After writing his first book, *The Arians of the Fourth Century*, Newman took his first trip abroad, visiting Rome and the Mediterranean with his close friend, Hurrell Froude, and Froude's father. After his companions had set out on their return trip to England, Newman returned to Sicily by himself. There he fell ill of a fever and nearly died, but once again illness was accompanied by grace and conversion.

The year 1833, after Newman's return from the Mediterranean, saw the start of what would become known as the Oxford Movement, in which Newman played a leading role. The Movement sought to bring the Church of England back to its apostolic roots, to give it an understanding of its own identity in the face of increasing government control and to try to rouse it against the liberalism of the day which was pervading it as a storm clouds over a sunny sky.

Newman's influence and leadership in the Oxford Movement came not only from his writing of *Tracts for the Times* and articles on various topics, but also from his Sunday afternoon sermons at St Mary's – those sermons which have since attained such fame even apart from the Oxford Movement.

In the course of his studies and writings, and especially because of his study of the Fathers of the Church, Newman's views about the Church continued to change and develop. The primitive Church was his ideal, but where was he to find that Church in his day? This question loomed large for him.

Newman was a man of deep and varied friendships. Scattered among and permeating the many duties of the years he spent at Oriel College are the many friends who, as he wrote in a poem, came to his door "unask'd, unhoped" (*VV*, 46), as well as members of his own family, with the joys and sorrows attendant on relationships between fallible human beings. At that time it seemed as if the spectre of death lay just around the corner and Newman suffered the loss of both friends and family members in those years. His youngest sister, Mary, died quite suddenly in 1828. She was barely nineteen years old. In 1836 he lost his closest friend, Hurrell Froude, and his own mother. Both, friendships and family relationships suffered because of his change of religious opinion and especially because of his later conversion, but some relationships lasted many years, weathering the tests of time and distance.

Meanwhile, in contrast with the controversies, writing, preaching and general hectic nature of his life in Oxford, was Newman's pastoral work at Littlemore, a hamlet outside of Oxford, which fell within the parochial jurisdiction of St Mary the Virgin. Littlemore was a poor village without church or school when Newman took over its care in 1828. In 1836 a new church was consecrated in its midst and just a short time later a schoolhouse was built under the supervision of Newman's curate, J. R. Bloxam. Newman spent Lent of 1840 living in Littlemore and he found it hard to return to Oxford that May. In addition to his regular liturgical duties and visiting the sick, he worked with the children, aided by his sisters, teaching them to sing even Gregorian chant. His catechism lesson on Sundays also attracted undergraduates and dons from Oxford who enjoyed the walk to Littlemore on a fine day. When the time came for Newman to step away from controversy and to seek God's will for himself in a more secluded life of prayer, fasting and study, it was to Littlemore he went and there he received an answer to his prayers.

Oriel College

I have this morning been elected fellow of Oriel College. I do not know how sufficiently to be grateful to God for so great mercy – and my joy and thanksgiving are so much purer, inasmuch as I feel that what I have obtained must be good for me, for I have continually petitioned for good.

LD I, 129, Letter to Elizabeth Newman, 12 April 1822.

Oriel College, the front quadrangle

It was not my own arm which got me the victory; there was One who supported me from above, and blessed my endeavours. To Him be all the praise.

LD I, 140, Letter to Mrs. Newman, 3 May 1822.

John Keble, engraving from the Richmond portrait

I sat next Keble yesterday at dinner, and, as I have heard him represented, he is more like an undergraduate than the first man in Oxford – so perfectly unassuming and unaffected in his manner.

LD I, 131, Letter to Charles Robert Newman, 13 April 1822.

Pusey was elected Fellow of Oriel College in 1823 and joined the efforts of the Oxford Movement at the end of 1833.

Dr Pusey was, to use the common expression, a host in himself; he was able to give a name, a form, and a personality, to what was without him a sort of mob; ... He was a man of large designs; he had a hopeful, sanguine mind; he had no fear of others; he was haunted by no intellectual perplexities.

Apo., 62.

E. B. Pusey

John Henry Newman

Newman wrote two days before his ordination to the diaconate (13 June 1824):

Make me Thy instrument ... make use of me, when Thou wilt, and dash me to pieces when Thou wilt. Let me, living or dying, in fortune and misfortune, in joy and sadness, in health & Sickness, in honour and dishonour, be Thine.

AW, 200.

Old St Clement's Church at the Plain

Sunday May 16 Today I have come to a most important determination. St Clement's Church is to be rebuilt – but, before beginning the subscriptions, it is proposed, … to provide a Curate, who shall be a kind of guarantee to the subscribers that every exertion will be made, when the Church is built, to recover the parish from meeting houses, and on the other hand alehouses, into which they have been driven for want of convenient Sunday worship. The curacy has been offered to me, and, after several days consideration, I have accepted it. The parish consisting of 1500 souls, is increasing, and likely to give much trouble. The only good objection against my taking it is my weakness of voice.

AW, 198–199.

Over Worton Church, Chipping Norton, Oxfordshire, where Newman preached his first sermon 23 June 1824

On 17 Oct. 1879 Charlotte Pearson, née Giberne, wrote to Newman: 'The first time I saw you was when I was staying with my sister Sarah [wife of Walter Mayers] at Worton, when you walked over from Oxford to breakfast [a distance of 18 miles!], and afterwards, standing by the fire, repeated those beautiful lines from Milman's Martyr of Antioch, which had only lately been published – "Brother, thou art gone before us, etc –" and my youthful imagination was struck with the beauty of holiness in so young a man.'

LD I, 172, FN 1.

New St Clement's Church (seen from Addison's Walk, Magdalen College) for the building of which Newman raised funds during his curacy

About ten days ago I began my visitation of the whole parish, going from house to house, asking the names, numbers, trades, where they went to church etc etc.

LD 1, 180, Letter to Mrs Newman, July 28, 1824.

St Alban Hall

[Whately] has done me the honour of appointing me Vice Principal [of St Alban Hall]. This ... is a post of considerable authority and responsibility. I am Dean, Tutor, Bursar and all – in his absence indeed, Principal.

LD I, 222, Letter to Mrs Newman, 29 March 1825.

Newman about his task as a tutor:

I feel I have a great responsibility laid upon my shoulders, and hope I shall be directed and strengthened to make use of the talents put into my hands. – It will be something if I can in any measure promote the cause of God and spread the influence of the Gospel of Christ, and I am willing (I trust) to spend my life in the cause.

LD I, 284, Letter to Elizabeth Newman, 29 April 1826.

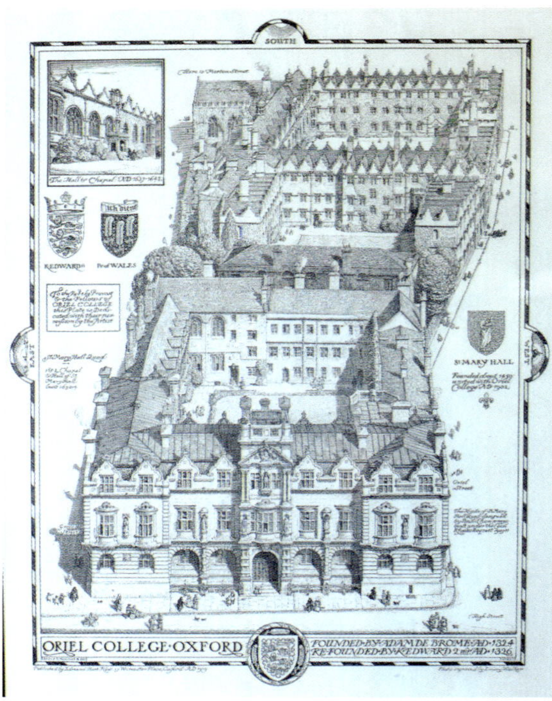

Oriel College, 1915–18

Richard Hurrell Froude, portrait as a boy – Hurrell Froude was elected Fellow of Oriel in 1826 and was a very close friend of Newman until his death ten years later

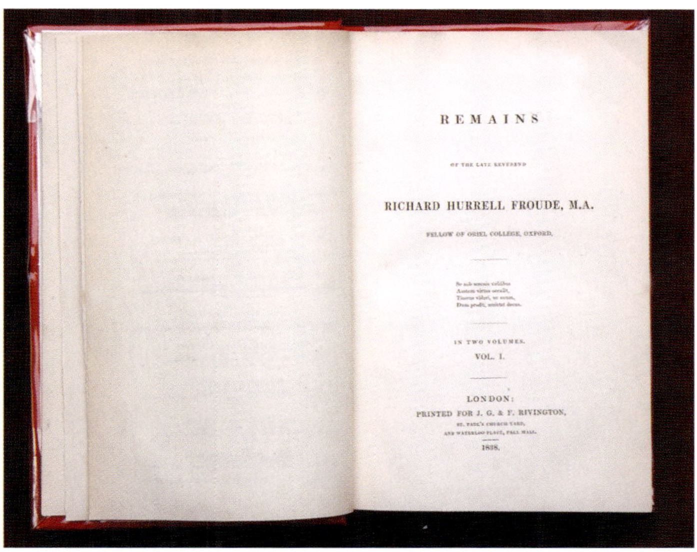

Froude's Remains – posthumously edited and published in two volumes by Newman and John Keble, 1836 and 1838 respectively

It is difficult to enumerate the precise additions to my theological creed which I derived from a friend to whom I owe so much. He taught me to look with admiration towards the Church of Rome, and in the same degree to dislike the Reformation. He fixed deep in me the idea of devotion to the Blessed Virgin, and he led me gradually to believe in the Real Presence.

Apo. 25.

Maria Rosina Giberne, met Newman in December 1826. She later followed him into the Catholic Church and they remained good friends the rest of her life

Mary Newman, John Henry's youngest sister, whose death on 5 January 1828 at the age of nineteen was a great blow for Newman

I need scarcely say, I should hope, how very much your very kind letter encouraged me. It could not do otherwise, and amid some opposition I do believe such testimony to the power of principles I hold is not without service to me. One wishes to have some proof that one is not dreaming; and your witness is like Gideon's fleece of wool.

LD V, 82, Letter to Miss M. R. Giberne, 21 June 1835.

Henry Wilberforce was Newman's private pupil for a short time in 1827, and remained one of his closest friends until his death in 1873

Well, my dear H, God bless you and may you keep well and be able to send good accounts of yourself – and feel that God is merciful and that while we are all sinners, yet no one must be scared or terrified who can calmly throw himself on His mercy.

LD V, 209, Letter to Henry Wilberforce, 21 January 1836.

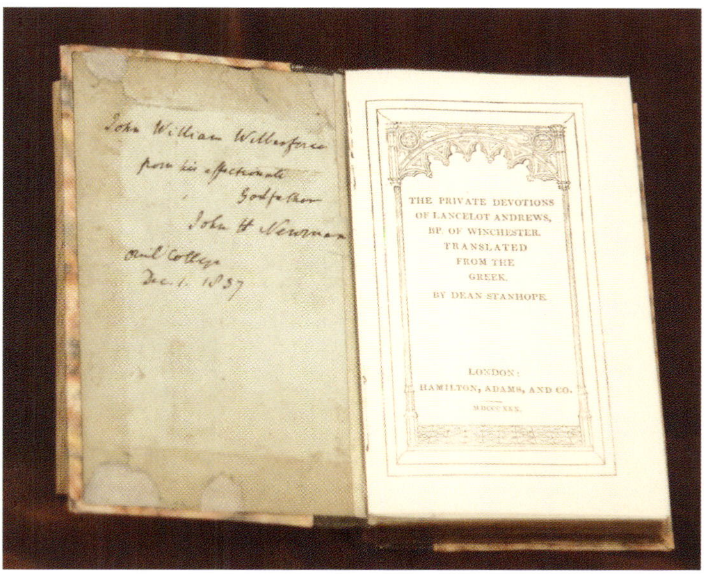

Book given by Newman to his Godson, John William Wilberforce, the son of Henry Wilberforce

The book is signed:

John William Wilberforce from his affectionate Godfather John H. Newman, Oriel College, Dec. 1. 1837.

May I be patient. It is so difficult to realize what one believes, and to make these trials, as they are intended, real blessings.

LD II, 66, Letter to Harriett Newman, 21 April 1828.

University Church of St Mary the Virgin seen from Radcliffe Square

In 1828 I became Vicar of St. Mary's. It was to me like the feeling of spring weather after winter; and, if I may so speak, I came out of my shell; I remained out of it till 1841.

Apo., 16.

Newman's sermons had the most wonderful effect on us young men. It was to many of us as if God had spoken to us for the first time. ... I do not see how this could have been, unless he who spoke was himself a seer, who saw God, and the things of God, and spoke that which he had seen, in the keen, bright, intuition of faith.... He had the wondrous, the supernatural power of raising the mind to God, and of rooting deeply in us a personal conviction of God, and a sense of His Presence.

William Lockhart, Cardinal Newman: Reminiscences of Fifty Years Since, London, 1891, 24, 26-27, as quoted in Positio, I, 95.

The pulpit from which Newman preached in the University Church of St Mary the Virgin

There was first the style, always simple, refined, and unpretending,..., but always marked by a depth of feeling which evidently sprang from the heart and experience of the speaker....I question whether, as suited to a University audience, England has ever known a preacher of equal power....

Memorials of William Charles Lake 1869-1894, *ed. Katharine Lake, London, 1901, 40-41, 50, as quoted in Positio, I, 94.*

So far is clear at once, that the preacher's object is the spiritual good of his hearers.

Idea, 406.

John Henry Newman, the preacher

A view in Sicily

Leonforte, Sicily, where Newman became seriously ill

Little as I have seen of Sicily, it has filled me with inexpressible delight and (in spite of dirt and other inconveniences) I am drawn to it as by a loadstone.

AW I, 344.

I hope it was not presumptuous, but from the beginning of my illness I had so strong a feeling on my mind that I should recover, that, whatever I did in the way of preparation for death (I mean, of giving my servant directions about letters etc) was done as a mere matter of duty. I could not help saying, 'I must act as if I were to die, but I think God has work for me yet.'

LD IV, 8, Letter to Henry Wilberforce, 16 July 1833.

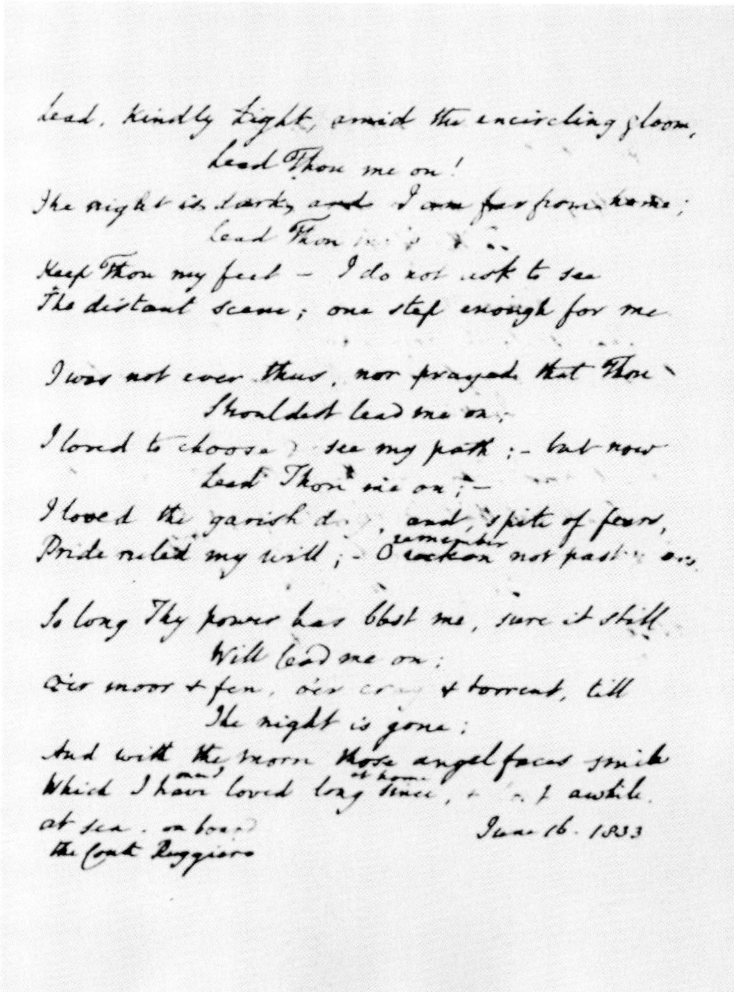
Lead, kindly Light, amid the encircling gloom,
Lead Thou me on!
The night is dark, and I am far from home;
Lead Thou me on.
Keep Thou my feet — I do not ask to see
The distant scene; one step enough for me.

I was not ever thus, nor prayed that Thou
Shouldst lead me on;
I loved to choose and see my path; — but now
Lead Thou me on; —
I loved the garish day, and, spite of fears,
Pride ruled my will; — O remember reckon not past years.

So long Thy power has blest me, sure it still
Will lead me on;
O'er moor and fen, o'er crag and torrent, till
The night is gone;
And with the morn those angel faces smile
Which I have loved long since, and lost awhile.
at sea. on board
the Conte Ruggiero
June 16. 1833

Lead, Kindly Light, in Newman's handwriting

I was aching to get home; yet for want of a vessel I was kept at Palermo for three weeks. I began to visit the Churches, and they calmed my impatience, though I did not attend any services. I knew nothing of the Presence of the Blessed Sacrament there. At last I got off in an orange boat, bound for Marseilles. Then it was that I wrote the lines "Lead, kindly light", which have since become well known.

Apo., 35.

The spire of the University Church of St Mary the Virgin seen from Oriel Lane – Newman began weekly early Eucharist there in 1837

Thought and word are one in the Eternal Logos, and must not be separate in those who are His shadows on earth. They must issue fresh and fresh, as from the preacher's mouth, so from his breast, if they are to be "spirit and life" to the hearts of his hearers.

Idea, 426.

Thus the Apostles tamed the pagan breast,
They argued not, but preach'd;
and conscience did the rest.

VV, 167, The Religion of Cain.

John Henry Newman, Vicar of St Mary the Virgin

This is our real and true bliss, not to know, or to affect, or to pursue; but to love, to hope, to joy, to admire, to revere, to adore. Our real and true bliss lies in the possession of those objects on which our hearts may rest and be satisfied. ... the thought of God, and nothing short of it, is the happiness of man.

PS V, 316, The Thought of God the Stay of the Soul.

Oriel College, 1675

In spite of my ingrained fears of Rome, and the decision of my reason and conscience against her usages, in spite of my affection for Oxford and Oriel, yet I had a secret longing love of Rome the Mother of English Christianity, and I had a true devotion to the Blessed Virgin, in whose College I lived, whose Altar I served, and whose Immaculate Purity I had in one of my earliest printed Sermons made much of.

Apo., 165.

The Newman window in Oriel College, detail

Nothing is more certain in matter of fact, than that some men do feel themselves called to high duties and works, to which others are not called. Why this is we do not know.... No one has any leave to take another's lower standard of holiness for his own. It is nothing to us what others are. If God calls us to greater renunciation of the world, and exacts a sacrifice of our hopes and fears, this is our gain, this is a mark of His love for us, this is a thing to be rejoiced in.

PS VIII, 30–31, Divine Calls.

Crest of Oriel College

Newman wrote about the influence of college life on an Oxford student:

There he forms friendships, there he spends his happiest days; and, whatever is his career there, brilliant or obscure, virtuous or vicious, in after years, when he looks back on the past, he finds himself bound by ties of gratitude and regret to the memories of his College life. ... The routine of duties and observances, the preachings and the examinations and the lectures, the dresses and the ceremonies, the officials whom he feared, the buildings or gardens that he admired, rest upon his mind and his heart, and the shade of the past becomes a sort of shrine to which he makes continual silent offerings of attachment and devotion.

HS III, 234.

His appearance was striking....his face remarkably like that of Julius Caesar.... there was an original force of character which refused to be moulded by circumstances, which was to make its own way, and become a power in the world; a clearness of intellectual perception, a disdain for conventionalities, a temper imperious and wilful, but along with it a most attaching gentleness, sweetness, singleness of heart and purpose. Both were formed by nature to command others....Credo in *Newmannum* was a common phrase at Oxford, and is still unconsciously the faith of nine-tenths of the English converts to Rome.

James Anthony Froude, 'Oxford Counter Reformation, Letters III', Short Studies on Great Subjects, Vol. V, London, 1907, pp. 196-197, as quoted in Positio, 90.

My God, Thou seest me; I cannot see myself. Were I ever so good a judge about myself, ever so unbiassed, and with ever so correct a rule of judging, still, from my very nature, I cannot look at myself, and view myself truly and wholly.

MD, 564-565.

Newman's window, Rose Mount, Rose Hill, Iffley, where Newman's mother and sisters lived 1830–1833, and where they fixed up a room for John Henry, which he used as a sort of vicarage for Littlemore nearby

I have so delightful a room at Rose Hill that I regret to go [to Devonshire to visit Froude], even on that score, having just got into it. From my easy chair (...) I see both St. Mary's and Iffley churches from opposite windows. It is too good for me. I think of the prophet's little deal table, chair and japanned candlestick.

LD II, 340–341,
Letter to Samuel Rickards, 4 July, 1831.

Weep not for me;
Be blithe as wont, nor tinge with gloom
The stream of love that circles home,
...
I still am near;
Watching the smiles I prized on earth,
Your converse mild, your blameless mirth;
...

VV, 40, A Voice from Afar.

Rose Bank, now called Grove House, Iffley Turn, where Newman's mother and sisters lived, 1833–1836, and where his mother died after a short illness

Thomas Mozley, a pupil of Newman, elected Fellow of Oriel College in 1829

Upon receipt of Newman's letter approving of his engagement to Harriett, Thomas Mozley wrote:

I have scarcely time to say anything, but if I had a day I could not express the delight your few lines afford me. ... I knew of course that I should only see a fresh example of your tenderness and affectionateness, but I hardly could calculate on such an expression of your opinion of me ... My father and mother and all my brothers and sisters cannot contain their joy at acquiring such a sister. *LD V, 322, FN 1.*

Harriett Newman married Thomas Mozley in 1836

Church of St Mary and St Nicholas, Littlemore

My Chapel [Littlemore] began yesterday, and the first stone is to be solemnly laid next week. It is to be roofed in by the end of October – the two builders ran each other £663 against £665, the surveyor beforehand reckoning on £650; so I hope I have got it at about the right sum. This takes in every thing of fitting up except the bell.

LD V, 100, Letter to Richard Hurrell Froude, 16 July 1835.

Memorial to Newman's mother, Jemima Newman, in the Church of St Mary and St Nicholas, Littlemore, for which she laid the first stone. The church under construction is shown in the background of the memorial

The Church of St Mary and St Nicholas and adjacent school, Littlemore

I have effected a great reform (for the time) in the girls' hands and faces – lectured with unblushing effrontery on the necessity of their keeping their work clean, and set them to knit stockings with all their might.

LD VII, 285, Letter to Mrs John Mozley, 1 April 1840.

J. R. Bloxam, Newman's curate at Littlemore for a time, oversaw the building of the school there and remained a lifelong friend of Newman

The children are vastly improved in singing – and now that the organ is mute, their voices are so thrilling as to make one sick with love.

LD VII, 261, Letter to J. R. Bloxam, 15 March 1840.

The Littlemore schoolhouse

The Church of St Mary and St Nicholas, Littlemore

Newman preached his last sermon as an Anglican, The Parting of Friends, *at the commemoration of the consecration of the Church of St Mary and St Nicholas in Littlemore, 25 September 1843. A friend who attended the service wrote about it to his wife:*

The service was at eleven, and, as, usual the chapel was decorated, with flowers upon the altar, in the windows above, ... and they were most beautiful as well as elegantly arranged. ... The officiating clergy were Newman (for the last time) Pusey, Copeland and Bowles. There was a Communion, and Newman preached his farewell sermon. It is easy to tell you these simple facts, but it would be no easy thing to convey to you any adequate impression of the whole scene, the crowd of friends from all parts, the half-mournful greetings, the extreme silence of the chapel, ..., the children with their new frocks and bonnets (Newman's parting gift). ... But the sermon I can never forget.... Newman's voice was low, but distinct and clear.... "And now, my friends, my dear friends," (here a long pause), "if you should be acquainted with any one who by his teaching, or by his writings, or by his sympathy has helped you or has seemed to understand you, or fell with you, &c. Oh! My friends (here a long pause), remember such an one and pray for him." [At the end of the sermon, Newman descended from the pulpit, took off his M.A. hood, and left it draped over the communion rails.] ... And thus the services of the greatest man of our times, the acutest and most laborious, and most energetic of the sons of the English Church is lost to us, he retires into lay communion. (E. Ballasis, *Memorials of Mr. Serjeant Bellasis, 1800–1873*, London 1895, second edition, pp. 63-5.)

Newman's academic hood which he wore for preaching

LD IX, 534-535, FN 5.

The College and the Convert

Chapter 4

The College and the Convert

(1842-1847)

In 1842 Newman moved to Littlemore, a tiny hamlet outside of Oxford, in which he had ministered because it belonged to the parish of St Mary the Virgin in Oxford. He had built a church for the people there and grown to love his ministry in the little village, so different from Oxford with its university atmosphere. He leased an old granary which had been converted into cottages, and stables which he had made into a library. Some friends and acquaintances came to live with him for a shorter or longer period of time and eventually they began to live by a sort of rule which gave an order to their day: prayer in common, meals, periods of silence, and so on. Newman spent the following years until 1845 in prayer, fasting and study with the single purpose of knowing God's will for himself within the Church.

This was a time at once happy and full of tension, the tension of an impending decision, the tension of an uncertain future, the tension of holding others, especially friends and those who looked to him for guidance, in suspense. "I am going through what must be gone through", he wrote to a friend (*LD* X, p. 412, Letter to Henry Edward Manning, 16 November 1844). It was especially the unsettling of his friends which caused him so much distress. To those who asked him outright about his situation, he replied with candour, feeling that forthrightness may be the best medicine to prevent shock when the actual move to the Roman Church took place. He tried the same medicine with his long-time friend, Pusey – who could hardly believe that Newman would really leave the Church of England – feeling that it would spare Pusey pain if he could get him to look the situation in the face.

In 1843 William Lockhart, one of Newman's companions at Littlemore, suddenly joined the Catholic Church. Because he felt responsible for this to some extent, but also because he had come to believe the Church of Rome to be the true Church of Christ, Newman resigned as Vicar of St Mary the Virgin, unwilling to continue as a minister in a communion which he felt to be in schism.

Newman remained in the Church of England as a layman for some time, still praying to know his way. He found some relief from the growing tension in writing letters about the development of his thought to Mrs William Froude. These letters give a good outline of Newman's intellectual development and it was surely a help to Newman to look back on the way he had come and to see more clearly where he was going. Yet when he tried to put down his process of reasoning in another letter he confessed that he could not do justice to the development which he had gone through. The impression had remained, though the reasoning leading to it had gone, "like a scaffolding taken down when the building is completed" (*LD* X, p. 376, Draft letter to unknown addressee, 30 October, 1844).

The conviction that the Church of England was in schism and that the Roman Church was the true Church had continued to grow on him and had reached such a point that he was getting afraid to travel for fear of an accident; he did not want to die outside the true Church. Still he did not yet feel the call to move. He felt he should test himself further. Though he could find no wrong motive in himself, he did not want to go by his feelings; he could not trust them. What if he was being somehow deceived? It was in this frame of mind that Newman began his *Essay on the Development of Christian Doctrine*. Hoping to remove the last remaining obstacles in his path, to clear away any intellectual clouds hanging over the Church of Rome, he began to investigate the theory of development in doctrine and to apply it to certain test doctrines. As he worked, the obstacles in his path were removed and the clouds dissipated. Before the book was finished he decided to be received into the Roman Catholic Church.

On 9 October 1845 John Henry Newman was received into the Catholic Church by Dominic Barberi (now Blessed), an Italian Passionist priest who had felt the call to work in England when he was very young and who had been following the progress of the

Oxford Movement with great hope. By the time he was received, most of the others staying with Newman at Littlemore had joined the Catholic Church. Two were received with him.

Newman stayed in Littlemore until February of 1846 and then moved for a short time to Old Oscott, renamed Maryvale, together with many of those who had been with him of Littlemore. At the urging of Dr. Wiseman, later Cardinal Archbishop of Westminster, Newman decided to become a Catholic priest, and was sent to Rome with Ambrose St John to complete his studies at the Propaganda Fide. He was ordained priest on 30 May 1847.

Newman had found his home at last. He never regretted his move to the Catholic Church, which he described as "coming into port after a rough sea" (*Apo.* p. 238) and the privileges of his new home, especially the presence of Our Lord in the Blessed Sacrament, outweighed all those he had lost and given up by his decision. Most of the others who began the Oxford Movement with him, Keble, Pusey, Church, Rogers, remained Anglican until their deaths. Bowden had died in 1844, still Anglican. Not one of Newman's immediate family followed him into the Catholic Church.

Several years after his conversion, Newman wrote of himself to a friend, "those sad long years of anxiety have stamped themselves on my face – and now that they are at an end, yet I cannot change what has become a physical effect. ... I will but add that the Hand of God is most wonderfully over me, that I am full of blessings and privileges, that I never have had even the temptation for an instant to feel a misgiving about the great step I took in 1845" (*LD* XII, p. 223, Letter to Mrs William Froude, 16 June 1848).

The cottages leased by Newman had been used as a granary for the Oxford and Cambridge Coach, and the library had been the stables.

... Costar's successors have turned his granary (at the corner going down to Humphries's) into cottages – We thought they would prove a great nuisance to the place and took them any how. Then I wanted room for my books, which now are actually covering the greater part of my floor in Oriel – so I got the Costar people to turn some stables adjacent into rooms, whither I hope to take my library in the course of a few weeks.

LD VIII, p. 418, Letter to Mrs. John Mozley, 9 January 1842.

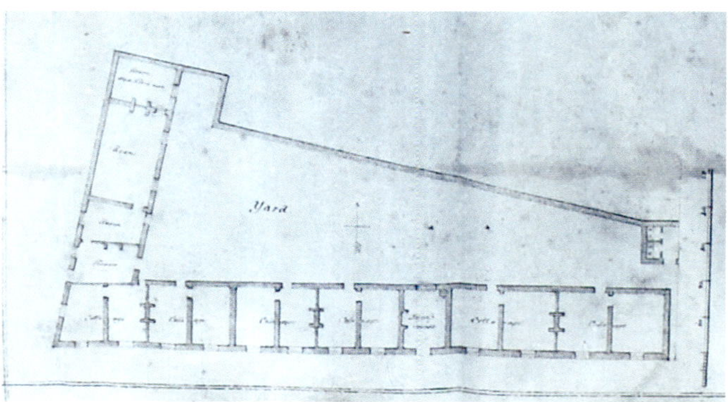

Plan of the cottages at Littlemore attached to Newman's lease

I am fitting up a very pretty little parsonage here, which as the summer gets on will look very nicely, I hope, though a good deal of money must first be laid out on it. I have got it on a lease for seven years with the option of continuing it for another seven. Harriett or Jemima will some day be giving you an account of it – but I shall be glad if they do not see it, till I get it in trim.

LD VIII, p. 470, Letter to Elizabeth Newman, 21 February 1842.

The College

Newman moved into his new home on 20 April 1842. Two days later he wrote:
I am just come here – and must set things going – and that requires close residence for a while. At this very moment I am literally solus without servant or any thing else – but I suppose we shall accumulate in time.

LD VIII, 508, Letter to J. W. Bowden, 22 April 1842.

Inside it is very pretty and neat – just my fancy. I do not wonder at John's present enthusiasm. There are 4 or 5 sets of rooms – sitting and bedroom – all on the ground floor – the door opening into the verandah which runs all along, a length of the diagonal of Oriel quad.

Newman Family Letters, 121, Letter from Harriett to Jemima, 13 May 1842.

"The Newman-Ooth College", a satirical print of Newman's supposed monastery

Newman explained to his bishop, who had heard different rumours about his new place of residence:

...no 'monastery' is in process of erection; there is no 'chapel', no 'refectory', hardly a dining room or parlour. The 'cloisters' are my shed connecting the cottages. ... I am attempting nothing ecclesiastical, but something personal and private.

LD VIII, 507, Letter to Richard Bagot, Bishop of Oxford, 14 April 1842.

Cottage No. 1, The College, which served as the guest room

Perhaps I might take one or two pupils who were reading for orders. Perhaps friends in orders might wish to come there for a while. Or I might have friends staying with me, as other clergymen receive their friends at their Parsonages. Sometimes there would be friends from Oxford. Your Lordship will think the building a very large one to admit of such prospective arrangements, but I am setting before you all my views, as far as I have any; and not knowing how or whether they will be fulfilled. There are six cottages of two rooms apiece, making 6 to 12 beds – and one additional room over the Library.

LD VIII, 506, Letter to Richard Bagot, Bishop of Oxford, 14 April 1842.

The College, Littlemore

Breviary and photograph of John Dobrée Dalgairns, the first friend to join Newman at his cottages in Littlemore

First let me advise you not to sit up late at night. It is not fair to yourself. Get up as early as you please. This too is really more Catholic!

LD IX, 160, Letter to J. D. Dalgairns, 26 November 1842.

William Lockhart

Perhaps you know already from your proximity to Loughborough, that Lockhart, who has been living here with me for a year past, has at Dr Gentili's at that place [*sic*], conformed to the Church of Rome. It has taken us all by surprise. He was away for three weeks with his Mother etc – and suddenly was overcome. So at least it appears. He was very near going over several years since – and, when he came here, I took a promise of him that he would remain quiet for three years – otherwise I could not receive him.

LD IX, 479, Letter to Mrs John Mozley, 28 August 1843.

Our Lady's Altar in the Passionist Monastery of S. Angelo di Vetralla

On the Apennines, near Viterbo, there dwelt a shepherd-boy, ... whose mind had early been drawn heavenward; and, one day, as he prayed before an image of the Madonna, he felt a vivid intimation that he was destined to preach the Gospel under the northern sky. ... Yet, though no external means appeared, the inward impression did not fade; on the contrary, it became more definite, and in process of time, instead of the dim north, England was engraven on his heart.

LG, 423.

He is a shrewd clever man, but as unaffected and simple as a child; and most singularly kind in his thoughts of religious persons in our communion. I wish all persons were as charitable as I know him to be. After waiting near 30 years, suddenly his Superiors sent him to England, without any act of his own. However, he has not laboured in conversions, but confined himself to missions and retreats among his own people. I believe him to be a very holy man.

LD XI, 5-6, Letter to Mrs J. W. Bowden, 8 October 1845.

Bl. Dominic Barberi

The Angel Hotel, High Street, Oxford, from where Dominic Barberi was fetched by John Dobreé Dalgairns the evening of 8 October 1845.

> I send you a hasty line, as I do to many others, to say that I am about to ask for admittance into the Catholic Church at the hands of Father Dominic the Passionist, who comes here tonight. He is on his way to Belgium, and does not know of my intention.
>
> *LD XI, 4, Letter to Edward Badeley, 8 October 1845.*

Blessed Dominic Barberi

Newman asks Dominic Barberi to hear his confession and to receive him into the Catholic Church

Father Dominic, the Passionist, came here last night - and though he was just off a trying journey, let me begin my Confession to him at once. He is now gone to Mass in Oxford - on his return I am to complete it; and, if it is so ordered, shall be received this evening into what I believe to be the One only Fold of Christ.

LD XI, 12, Letter to William Dodsworth, 9 October 1845.

The fireplace depicted in the library today. It was before the fire at this spot that Dominic Barberi stood drying himself late in the evening of 8 October 1845 when Newman came in, knelt before him and asked to be received into the Catholic Church.

The desk Newman used at Littlemore and on which he wrote An Essay on the Development of Christian Doctrine. *It had originally belonged to Henry Wilberforce*

"I have brought here your little reading desk …. I had not the heart to let it remain behind. … It formed part of the altar on which Fr Dominic offered mass, and from which I received my first communion. … Please come and fetch it."

LD XI, 129. Letter to Henry Wilberforce, 26 February 1846.

Relics of Bl. Dominic Barberi in Newman's bedroom today

Exterior of the Church of St Ignatius, at St Clements, Oxford

It is said that the one support to persons in my case has been the daily Mass – now mass is only twice a week at St Clement's, and at the distance of 2 or 3 miles. Nor is it a slight trial, as you may suppose, except as faith overcomes it, to go to what to outward appearance is a meeting house.

LD XI, 16, Letter to Mrs John Mozley, 14 October 1845.

Interior of the Church of St Ignatius, at St Clements, Oxford

Newman's private room as it is today

Newman's room at The College as it is presented today. The writing utensils on the desk belonged to Newman, and both the floor and the fireplace are original to the room

As you suppose, it was of course a very trying thing to quit Littlemore – I quite tore myself away – and could not help kissing my bed, and mantlepiece, and other parts of the house.

LD XI, 132, Letter to W. J. Copeland, 10 March 1846.

Littlemore as depicted in the Newman window in Oriel College

Another comfort amid the pain of quitting this place, is the pleasant memory which attaches to it. In spite of my having been in such doubt and suspense, it has been the happiest time of my life, because so quiet. Perhaps I shall never have such quiet again.

LD XI, 126, Letter to Mrs J. W. Bowden, 22 February 1846.

Yesterday I was here quite alone – as I came into the house by myself four years ago, so I have left by myself. This afternoon I dine with Manuel, sleeping there – tomorrow morning, if all is well, I go off to my new home.

LD XI, 125, Letter to Mrs J. W. Bowden, 22 February 1846.

The Oxford Observatory. Here Newman spent his last night in Oxford with his friend Manuel Johnson

Manuel Johnson

You are ever in my thoughts – no one is there I think of more tenderly – for you were so kind to us all at Oxford, and we seem so ungrateful in leaving you.

LD XI, 198, Letter to Manuel Johnson, 8 July 1846.

John Henry Newman and Ambrose St John studying at Propaganda Fide, with Our Lady of the Miraculous Medal in the background

We are treated as if we were princes, much to our distress. … It is really quite absurd, considering our habits, but they will not believe we like plainer things, and are surprised to find we can bear in daily things to do as they do. They insist on our having tea at night, and are always anticipating our wishes.

LD XI, 272, 273, Letter to Mrs J. W. Bowden, 15 November 1846.

Chapel of Propaganda Fide, Rome, where Newman celebrated his first Mass

...Christ's priests have no priesthood but His. They are merely his shadows and organs, they are His outward signs; and what they do, He does; when they baptize, He is baptizing; when they bless, He is blessing. He is in all acts of His Church, and one of its acts is not more truly His act than another, for all are His.

PS VI, 242, Waiting for Christ.

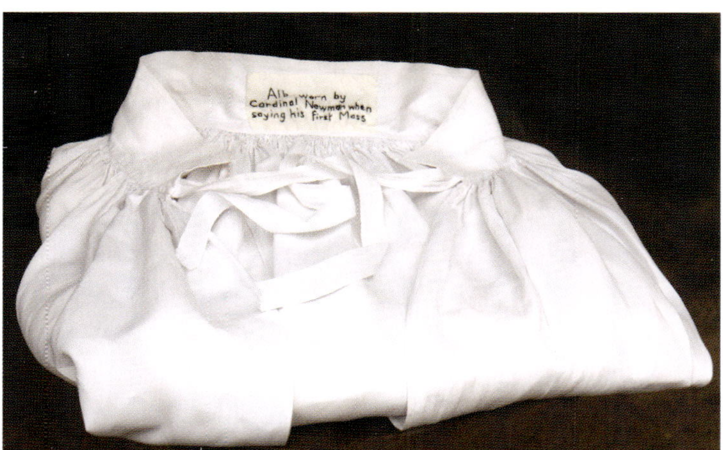

Alb in which Newman is supposed to have celebrated his first Mass on the Solemnity of Corpus Christi 1847

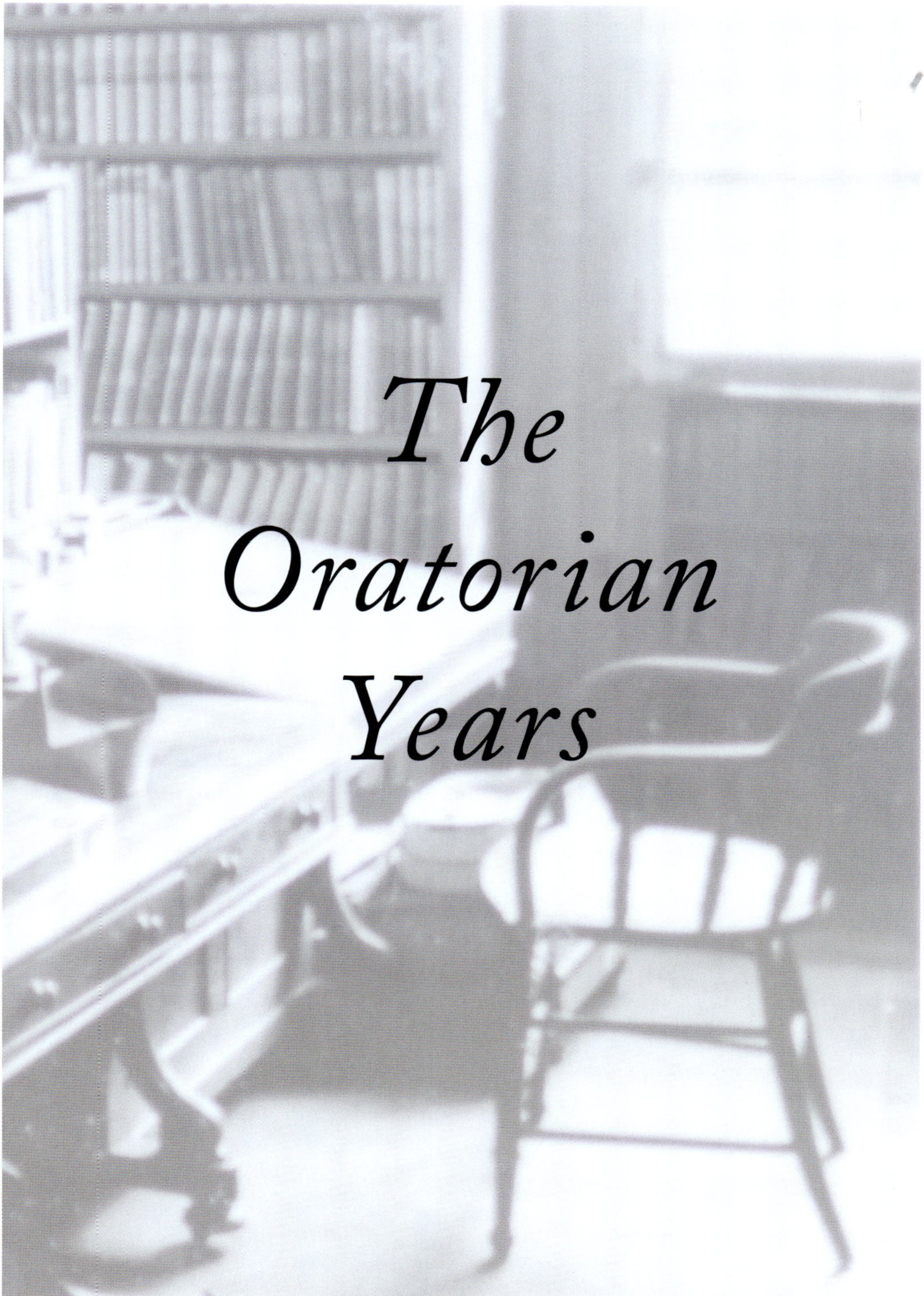

The Oratorian Years

Chapter 5

The Oratorian Years

(1847-1879)

Papal approval of the plan to introduce the Oratory of St Philip Neri into England was received on 21 February (Newman's birthday) 1847. It was decided that after their ordination to the priesthood, Newman, St John and the others with them would make their novitiate in Rome under an Oratorian Father. This took place during the summer and autumn of 1847. Newman and St John returned to England on Christmas Eve of the same year. On 1 February 1848 Newman established the first English Oratory in Maryvale, and two weeks later admitted F. W. Faber and his companions at St Wilfrid's to the Oratory.

A year after its founding, Newman moved the Oratory to Alcester Street in Birmingham, where they had bought and rebuilt an old gin distillery to fit their needs. In June of that same year, the Oratory in London was founded, with Faber as superior and many of his followers as members. In 1852, three years after its founding, the Birmingham Oratory was moved again, this time to its present site in Edgbaston, Birmingham.

Having found his home in the Oratory, Newman settled into the life of an Oratorian priest with its pastoral demands of hearing confessions, preaching, and visiting the sick. In addition, it was up to him, as superior, to hold the monthly chapter meetings, which involved giving a talk to his fellow Oratorians. There seemed to be nearly always some building work or other going on in or for the Oratory and Newman had to look after such practical matters as well. Of course, he had the help of his fellow Oratorians, especially Fr Ambrose St John, who had been his faithful friend since his Littlemore days. Newman nonetheless found time for writing, for giving several series of lectures and, in later years, for republishing his Anglican works with his own comments as a Catholic.

In 1851, while delivering the fifth lecture in a series "On the Present Position of Catholics in England", Newman denounced the ex-priest Giovanni Giacinto Achilli, who had lived an immoral life and abused women, and who then came to England and gave lectures against the Catholic Church. Achilli, thinking Newman could not produce evidence for his statements, sued him for libel. The case dragged on for two years with the judge finding in favour of Achilli, in a decision which was recognized even by Protestants to be biased. Newman was fined £100.

Newman was not idle while the trial was in progress. In addition to doing what he could for his case and asking prayers from the Catholic world, for he was convinced that only prayer could save the situation for the Church, and in addition to his normal duties as an Oratorian and as superior of the house, he began a project which was as dear to his heart as it was difficult and trying. In November 1851, Newman was asked to set up and to serve as the first rector of the Catholic University of Ireland in Dublin, a post he held until 1857. To prepare for the opening of the University, Newman gave his lectures on university education which, after their publication in a third edition, became known as the *Idea of a University*, one of Newman's most celebrated and most widely read works.

In October 1850, Msgr Wiseman had announced the restoration of the hierarchy in England. The first synod of bishops of the restored hierarchy took place in July 1852. Newman preached his sermon, "The Second Spring", for the occasion. This was while the Achilli libel case was proceeding.

November 1853 saw the opening of the Oratory Church in Birmingham and November 1854 the opening of the Catholic University in Dublin. To the university buildings Newman added a church, designed by the architect John Hungerford Pollen and paid for with money left over from the contributions made by Catholics to pay for the expenses of the Achilli case. Newman dedicated his *Idea of a University* to those who had so generously supported him in the trial; he had, in fact, received donations and prayerful support from Catholics around the world.

Newman resigned as rector of the Catholic University in Ireland in 1857. In six years he had crossed the Irish Sea some 56 times, working to maintain the University, while remaining superior of the Birmingham Oratory and, for the first year, appearing on trial in the libel case against him. After his resignation, he threw himself even more into pastoral work and work for the Oratory, founding the Oratory School in May 1859.

In 1864 the novelist, Charles Kingsley attacked Newman's honesty and the honesty of all Catholic clergy in an article. After a correspondence with Kingsley in which he did not get a satisfactory apology or retraction, Newman wrote his celebrated *Apologia pro vita sua* to lay before the world the evolution of his mind in the question of religion. The *Apologia* catapulted Newman once again into the limelight and brought many, Catholics and Anglicans alike, to see the honesty of his motives and the integrity of the man.

In the autumn of 1865 E. B. Pusey published a book which he hoped would be a step towards peace between the Anglican and Catholic churches. He called it, therefore, *An Eirenicon*. In it he wrote that the two main difficulties existing between the two communions were the Catholic 'worship' of the Blessed Virgin Mary and the infallibility of the Pope as understood by Catholics. He used some of Newman's Anglican works to defend his thesis. Newman decided to answer his old friend and published his *Letter to Pusey* in January 1866. It contains some of Newman's most clear and rich thoughts on devotion to the Blessed Virgin Mary.

In 1870 Newman published his *Essay in Aid of a Grammar of Assent*, a book which had been in his mind for many years and which took many attempts to get on paper. In it he sought to show what assent is, how the mind reaches it and that faith is a certitude.

The proclamation of the dogma of infallibility of the Pope at the First Vatican Council called forth various fears and prejudices among non-Catholics. So it was that in 1875 Gladstone, the English Prime Minister, wrote that Catholics could not be loyal subjects of the Crown because they are bound to believe and obey the Pope. Newman replied in *A Letter to the Duke of Norfolk* which articulated his celebrated understanding of conscience.

That same year Ambrose St John died. It was a grievous loss to

Newman and to the Birmingham Oratory. Newman felt that his death had left a wound in him which might not ever heal. Later he attributed the influx of four novices to the Birmingham Oratory to St John, who while on earth was so anxious to have vocations for the Oratory.

Newman's Oratorian years, speaking now of those before he was made a Cardinal, were years of full activity. They were not easy years; on the contrary, they were filled with trials of every kind and in every sphere of life. Newman learned well how to distinguish between the human and divine elements in the Church. He was not blind to the human foibles, weaknesses and errors of those in ecclesiastical office, but they never dimmed his great love for the Church or clouded his faith in her. He suffered greatly as a Catholic at the hands of Catholics, but he had found his home, both in the Roman Catholic Church and in the Oratory. He was in peace. Many of his contemporaries attest to his strength of character, his cheerfulness, his perseverance in the face of adversity and, above all, to his great humility.

St Philip Neri celebrating Mass in the catacombs of St Sebastian

St Philip... founded his Congregation in charity – making it the distinguishing mark by which his children were different from regulars, that what regulars did from observance of the sanctity of their vow, the Oratorian was to do from love. Love was to stand in the place of vows.

NO, 222.

External mortification, as has been already said, is *not* the mark of an Oratorian, but *internal;* or in other words, mortification of his private judgment, and his own will.

NO, 403.

St Philip's death mask

Engraving of Old Oscott, Newman's 'Maryvale'

By our authority we appoint John Henry Newman superior of his House of the Oratory at Maryvale and of the one to be erected in the city of Birmingham.

From the Apostolic Brief of His Holiness Pope Pius IX, Positio Super Virtutibus, *189.*

"We are at last a Congregation. I admitted nine after first Vespers of the Purification. We are six Fathers, one novice, three lay brothers."

LD XII, 165, Letter to Mrs J. W. Bowden, 3 February 1848.

Our Lady of Victory in the chapel of Maryvale, where The Oratory was set up after Solemn Vespers on 1 February 1848

Fragments, extracts, specimens, convey no idea to the world of what we are; he who wishes to know us must condescend to study us. The Catholic doctrine is after all too great to be comfortably accommodated in a Protestant nutshell; it cannot be surveyed at a glance, or refuted by a syllogism.

Prepos, 150.

John Henry Newman in 1851, giving his Discourses on the Present Position of Catholics in England at the Corn Exchange in Birmingham

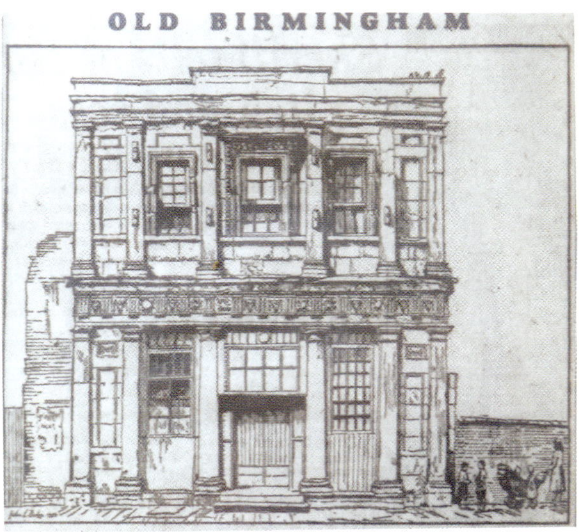

The first Oratory in Alcester Street

Service (morning) just over – chapel full – crammed – but not a good collection ... We expect a row this evening, and are sending for two policemen.

LD XIII, 21, Letter to F.W. Faber, 4 February 1849.

We are in a very anxious crisis [the Achilli Trial] … I have no confidence in any of those who had to do with the matter before - but I have the greatest confidence in the multitude of Masses and prayers which have been said for me.

LD XV, 23, Letter to J. Butt,
23 January 1852.

Unfinished painting of the first Synod of the new Province of Westminster

To set up the Church again in England is too great an act to be done in a corner. We have had reason to expect that such a boon would not be given to us without a cross. It is not God's way that great blessings should descend without the sacrifice first of great sufferings. If the truth is to be spread to any wide extent among this people, how can we dream, how can we hope, that trial and trouble shall not accompany its going forth?

SVO, 178, "The Second Spring".

Chapel of St Mary's College, Oscott. Here Newman preached his famous sermon, "The Second Spring" on 13 July 1852

Paul Cardinal Cullen (1803-1878), who asked Newman to become the Rector of the proposed Catholic University of Ireland

It is my happiness in a matter of Christian duty, about which the most saintly and the most able may differ, to be guided simply by the decision and recommendation of the Holy See, the judge and finisher of all controversies. ... My sole aspiration – and I cannot have a higher under the heavens – is to be the servant of the Vicar of Christ.

Discourses on the Scope and Nature of University Education, 19.

John Hungerford Pollen on his time with Newman in Dublin:

As for his 'gaiety of heart' it shed cheerfulness as a sunbeam sheds light, even while many difficulties were pressing ... What a time it was! Reading, thinking, writing, working, walking with him in the hours of recreation over the pleasant lawns; listening to talk that was never didactic and never dull; refreshing after the toils of the day as running waters.

'Newman in Dublin', The Month *(September 1906), 320.*

Newman House, St Stephen's Green, the original location of the Catholic University of Ireland

Aubrey de Vere described Newman as follows:

Another most remarkable union in Newman of qualities commonly opposed to each other, was that of a dauntless courage with profound thoughtfulness. ... In Newman there existed the rare union of the contemplative mind and the heroic soul.

Recollections of Aubrey de Vere, *E. Arnold, New York and London, 1897: Positio, 270.*

Entrance porch of the University Church, Dublin

Newman wrote about the building of the church, a project he realised with John Hungerford Pollen:

"I thought – (1) Nothing was a more simple and complete advertisement than a large Church open for worship, the cheapest advertisement, since, if self-supporting, it cost the University nothing, yet was perpetual and in the face of the day. (2) It symbolized the great principle of the University, the indissoluble union of philosophy with religion. (3) It provided for University formal acts, for Degree-giving, for solemn lectures and addresses ...

Campaign, 290.

Interior of the University Church, Dublin

Newman's teapot

Let us day by day, let us, when we rise in the morning, make an offering of ourselves to Him.

NO, 347.

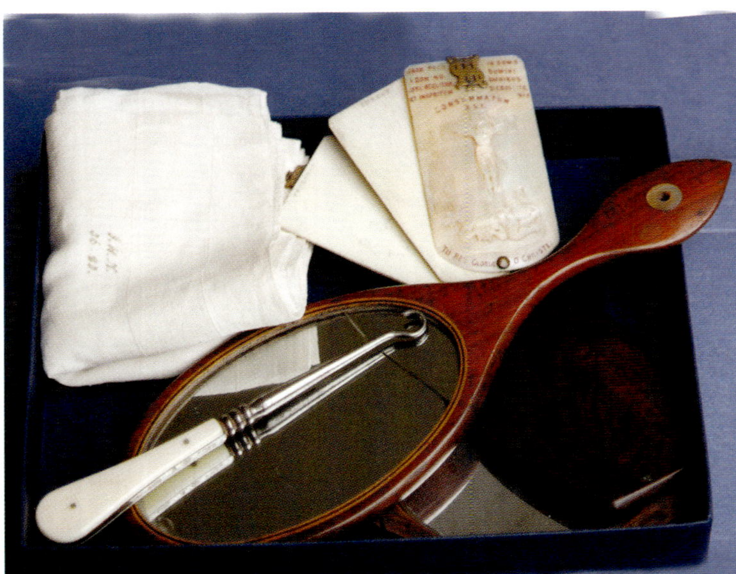

Newman's shaving mirrors, boot hook, handkerchief, and pocket diary

Newman at the Oratory, 1861

The Congregation of the Oratory, then, is a community of secular priests, living together without vows, for the fulfilment of their ministry, under a rule and with privileges given them by the Holy See.

NO, 314.

Let it be our aim then, my Fathers and Brothers, that every fresh moment, that every chapter, at it comes, may find us more and more in our place, more and more at home, more and more in possession of our true relations to things about us and a good understanding with our duties. ... To us is entrusted the high and onerous office, of forming the character, of starting the traditions, of an infant Institution; and while St Philip's own idea is our only pattern, so his glorious intercession on high, and our own anxious prayers and jealous diligence, and the blessing of Almighty God and His dear Mother are our only means.

NO, 287-288.

It is a call on every one of us, not as simply the better way, but as a matter of life and death to our body, to cherish a personal affection for its [sic] other, and to show each other all kind, attentive, and humble service; and in this our great duty the difference between Superior and subjects, young and old, simply vanishes – for we live then only if we submit ourselves to each other, think others better than ourselves and are ever willing to take the lowest place, forgetting self.

NO, 375.

The present Oratory School in Woodcote near Reading

... if I could believe it to be God's will, [I] would turn away my thoughts from ever writing any thing, and should see, in the superintendence of these boys, the nearest return to my Oxford life – for, to my surprise, I find that Oxford 'men' and schoolboys are but varieties of one species, and I think I should get on with the one as I got on with the other ...

LD XXI, 51, Letter to Emily Bowles, 13 February 1864.

Newman in 1861

What I had meant to say then, to ask of Thee then, I ask of Thee now. ... I have asked it often in time past, I think, long before I was a Catholic! ... Now then let me make it once again. O Lord, bless what I write and prosper it - let it do much good, let it have much success; but let no praise come to me on that account in my lifetime. Let me go on living, let me die, as I have hitherto lived.

AW, 252, 8 January 1860.

Thirty years have passed since I have been a sort of target for a shot, when any one wished to try his hand, and had nothing better to do. I used as a Protestant, to say, that no one, except O'Connell was so well abused as I was. I have very seldom *replied*; if so, for the sake of others, or of our cause. ... Gross misrepresentations remain of me to this day, ... , knowing that *they* can speak, and *I* cannot.

LD XX, 29, Letter to Sr Mary Gabriel du Boulay, 18 August 1861.

Newman in 1864

Frederick William Faber

He said that a sermon of mine at St Mary's had been the turning point of his life – for it gave him the first notion he had of supernatural grace.

LD XVII, 559, Memorandum of his last meeting with F.W. Faber on 20 July 1863.

John Henry Newman's library in the Birmingham Oratory

August 31. My letter has been stopped – first by my great day-long doings in the library. I have been dusting, arranging, and re-arranging to an heroic degree, tho' I have not yet done all.

LD XX, 512, Letter to Ambrose St John, 26 August 1863.

John Henry Newman, 1864, the year when he wrote his Apologia

When I was at Oxford, I have twice written a pamphlet in a night, and once in a day – but now I had writing and printing upon me at once, and I have done a book of 562 pages, all at a heat; but with so much suffering, ... such long spells of work, sometimes 16 hours, once 22 hours at once, that it is a prodigious awful marvel that I have got through it, and that I am not simply knocked up by it. I am sure it is the prayers of my friends, which have sustained me, and you must go on praying that I may not feel the bad effects of such a strain on me afterwards.

LD XXI, 131, Letter to Sr Mary Gabriel du Boulay, 25 June 1864.

Newman wrote to a lady who was preparing to be received into the Church:

It is no sin to feel it difficult to accommodate your mind to certain things, and it is better not, in the way of devotions, to force yourself at all – though if you found you could without discomfort use the Rosary (five decades) daily, it would be good. In that case (I would send you a blest Rosary).

LD XXI, 387, Letter to Lavinia Wilson, 14 January 1865.

Newman's rosary

Henry Edward Cardinal Manning.

Manning's rise is marvellous – in fourteen years a Protestant Archdeacon is made Catholic Archbishop of Westminster, with the whole body of old Catholics, Bishops and all, under him.

LD XXI, 471, Letter to Robert Ornsby, 20 May 1865.

Sr Maria Pia (Maria Giberne)

What you say of your own difficulty in meditation, is quite what I should say of myself, if that is any comfort to you. I think the mind is weakened as one gets old, and cannot hold an idea any more than the muscles can hold a heavy weight. And then again, as the eyes get dim and the hearing dull, so in like manner the affections do not act in sensible emotions as they do when people are young. All this is very painful, and unsatisfactory – but I trust it is not a sign of falling back.

LD XXI, 480, Letter to Miss M. R. Giberne, end of May 1865 .

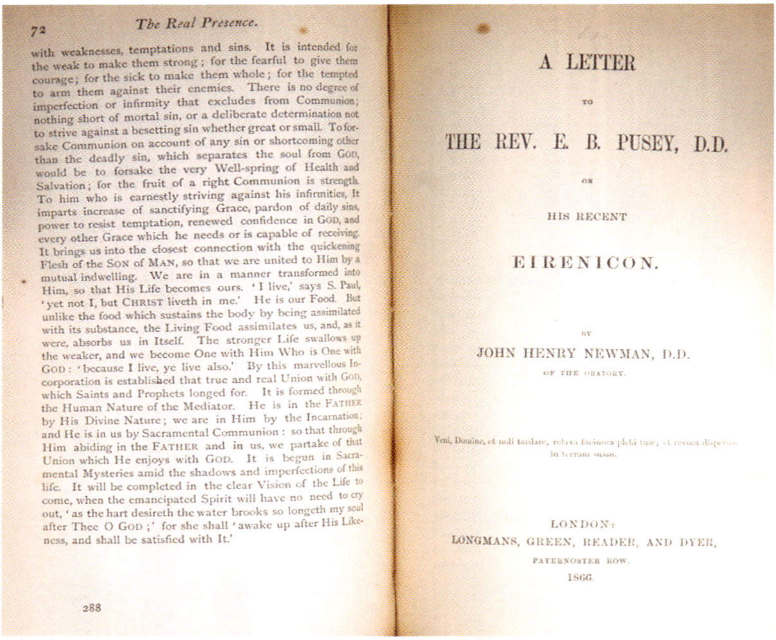

72 *The Real Presence.*

with weaknesses, temptations and sins. It is intended for the weak to make them strong; for the fearful to give them courage; for the sick to make them whole; for the tempted to arm them against their enemies. There is no degree of imperfection or infirmity that excludes from Communion; nothing short of mortal sin, or a deliberate determination not to strive against a besetting sin whether great or small. To forsake Communion on account of any sin or shortcoming other than the deadly sin, which separates the soul from God, would be to forsake the very Well-spring of Health and Salvation; for the fruit of a right Communion is strength. To him who is earnestly striving against his infirmities, It imparts increase of sanctifying Grace, pardon of daily sins, power to resist temptation, renewed confidence in God, and every other Grace which he needs or is capable of receiving. It brings us into the closest connection with the quickening Flesh of the Son of Man, so that we are united to Him by a mutual indwelling. We are in a manner transformed into Him, so that His Life becomes ours. 'I live,' says S. Paul, 'yet not I, but Christ liveth in me.' He is our Food. But unlike the food which sustains the body by being assimilated with its substance, the Living Food assimilates us, and, as it were, absorbs us in Itself. The stronger Life swallows up the weaker, and we become One with Him Who is One with God: 'because I live, ye live also.' By this marvellous Incorporation is established that true and real Union with God, which Saints and Prophets longed for. It is formed through the Human Nature of the Mediator. He is in the Father by His Divine Nature; we are in Him by the Incarnation; and He is in us by Sacramental Communion: so that through Him abiding in the Father and in us, we partake of that Union which He enjoys with God. It is begun in Sacramental Mysteries amid the shadows and imperfections of this life. It will be completed in the clear Vision of the Life to come, when the emancipated Spirit will have no need to cry out, 'as the hart desireth the water brooks so longeth my soul after Thee O God;' for she shall 'awake up after His Likeness, and shall be satisfied with It.'

288

A LETTER

TO

THE REV. E. B. PUSEY, D.D.

ON

HIS RECENT

EIRENICON.

BY

JOHN HENRY NEWMAN, D.D.

OF THE ORATORY.

Veni, Domine, et noli tardare, relaxa facinora plebi tuae; et revoca dispersos in terram suam.

LONDON:

LONGMANS, GREEN, READER, AND DYER,

PATERNOSTER ROW.

1866.

Letter to Pusey *in response to Pusey's* Eirenicon

However, as to all statements, I fear I must repeat what I have said before, that it is a first principle, which no one can hope to put aside, that with us the Pope is the centre of unity, 'totius Ecclesiae caput et omnium Christianorum Pater et Doctor,' and that he has a universal jurisdiction.

LD XXIII, 285, Letter to E. B. Pusey, 4 August 1867.

E. B. Pusey

John Henry Newman, plaster copy of the bust by Thomas Woolner

As I was not the best sitter in the world, I am glad to have your judgment that the anxious pains, which Mr Woolner took with me, are not likely to be thrown away.

LD XXII, 259–260, Letter to Francis Turner Palgrave, 15 July 1866.

We, the undersigned, have been deeply pained at some anonymous attacks which have been made upon you. They may be of little importance themselves, but we feel that every blow that touches you inflicts a wound upon the Catholic Church in this country. We hope, therefore, that you will not think it presumptuous in us to express our gratitude for all we owe you, and to assure you how heartily we appreciate the services which, under God, you have been the means of rendering to our Holy Religion.

LD XXIII, 139 FN 3, from a letter by a group of Catholic laymen, published in the Tablet, *13 April 1867.*

John Henry Newman, 1867

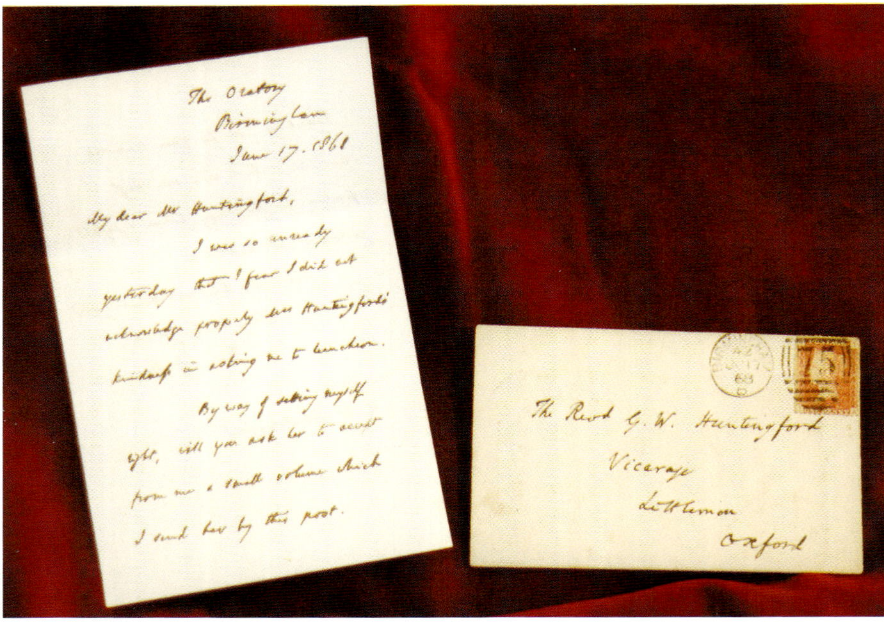
The Oratory
Birmingham
June 17. 1868

My dear Mr Huntingford,
I was so unready
yesterday that I fear I did not
acknowledge properly Mrs Huntingford's
kindness in asking me to luncheon.
By way of setting myself
right, will you ask her to accept
from me a small volume which
I send her by this post.

The Revd G. W. Huntingford
Vicarage
Littlemore
Oxford

Letter of John Henry Newman to Revd G. W. Huntingford

Newman wrote to the Vicar of Littlemore having visited the village for the first time after a gap of 22 years:

The Oratory
Birmingham
June 17, 1868

My dear Mr Huntingford,

I was so unready yesterday that I fear I did not acknowledge properly Mrs Huntingsford's kindness in asking me to luncheon.

By way of setting myself right, will you ask her to accept from me a small volume which I send by this post.

Thanking you for your various civilities, which were one chief feature in the happy hours I passed yesterday at Littlemore

I am, My dear Mr Huntingford Very truly Yours

John Henry Newman

LD XXIV, 88, Letter to Revd G. W. Huntingford, 17 June 1868.

Newman wrote about his Essay in Aid of a Grammar of Assent, *which was eventually published in 1870:*

The book itself I have aimed at writing these twenty years; - & now that it is written I do not quite recognize it for what it was meant to be, though I suppose it is such. I have made more attempts at writing it, than I can enumerate.

AW, 269.

Newman expressed his gratitude towards his close friend in the Apologia*:*

And to you especially, dear AMBROSE ST. JOHN; whom God gave me, when He took every one else away; who are the link between my old life and my new; who have now for twenty-one years been so devoted to me, so patient, so zealous, so tender; who have let me lean so hard upon you; who have watched me so narrowly; who have never thought of yourself, if I was in question.

Apo, 283.

Ambrose St John

Henry Wilberforce

Newman wrote in his letter of condolence to Henry's son upon his father's death:

Of course I shall say Masses for his soul; but I wish and pray that each of us, when our time comes, may as little need them as I think he does. None of us are fit to enter God's Holy Presence, but he has been preparing himself for it all through his life.

LD XXVI, 296, Letter to Wilfrid Wilberforce, 23 April 1873.

What a strange number of deaths of friends has marked this year! at least to me. Sam Wilberforce is the last – I call him Sam, because it recalls old days. I never knew him well, but I have before me quite clearly the vision of his coming up to residence at Oriel in 1832, leaning on Robert's arm.

LD XXVI, 341-342, Letter to John Hungerford Pollen, 23 July 1873.

Samuel Wilberforce, Bishop of Oxford

John Henry Newman, engraving of a drawing by Lady Coleridge

Lady Coleridge did three portraits of Newman. After having received one of them, Newman wrote:

I will not let an hour pass without thanking you and Lady Coleridge for your wonderfully kind and beautiful present, which has come quite safely. I hope she understands already, without my written words, how deeply I have felt her bountiful bestowal on me of her time and pains, her zeal and her genius – and, now, she has put the crown on her munificence by sending to us here its result.

LD XXVIII, 198, Letter to Lord Coleridge, 17 May 1877.

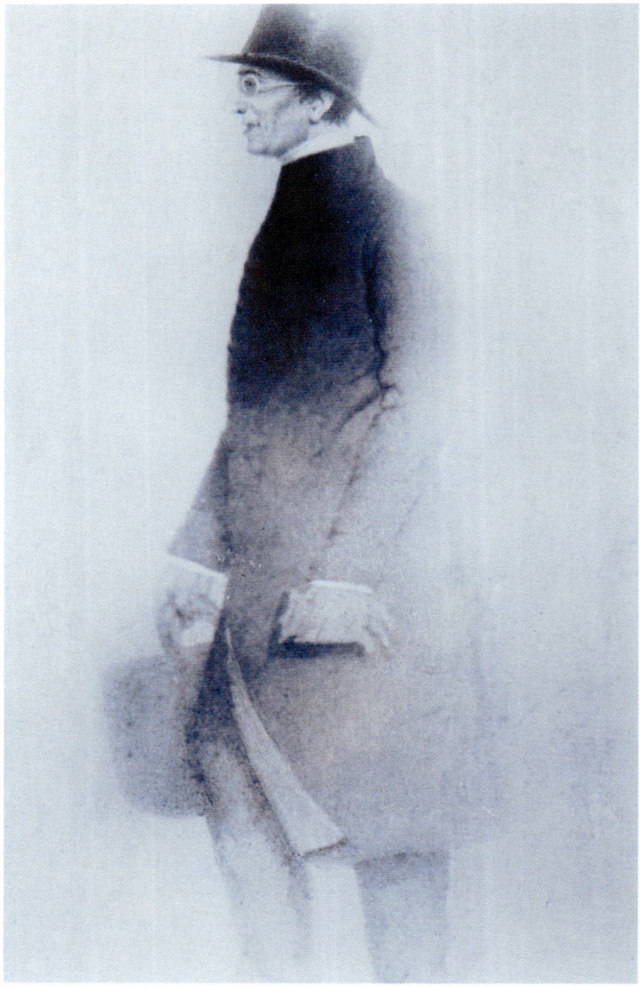

I looked, and then, I saw him passing along in his characteristic way, walking fast, without any dignity of gait but earnest, like one who had a purpose; yet so humble and self-forgetting in every portion of his external appearance, that you would not have thought him, at first sight, a man remarkable for anything. It was only when you came to know him that you recognised or began to recognise what he was.

William Lockhart, Cardinal Newman. Reminiscences of Fifty Years Since, *London, 1891, 1.*

God beholds thee individually, whoever thou art. He "calls thee by thy name." He sees thee, and understands thee, as He made thee. He knows what is in thee, all thy own peculiar feelings and thoughts, thy dispositions and likings, thy strength and thy weakness. He views thee in thy day of rejoicing, and thy day of sorrow. He sympathises in thy hopes and thy temptations. ... He compasses thee round and bears thee in his arms; He takes thee up and sets thee down. He notes thy very countenance, whether smiling or in tears, whether healthful or sickly. ... Thou dost not love thyself better than He loves thee. Thou canst not shrink from pain more than He dislikes thy bearing it; and if He puts it on thee, it is as thou would put it on thyself, if thou art wise, for a greater good afterwards. Thou art not only His creature ..., thou art man redeemed and sanctified, His adopted son ... Thou wast one of those for whom Christ offered up His last prayer, and sealed it with His precious blood.

PS III, 124-125, A Particular Providence as Revealed in the Gospel.

The Cardinal

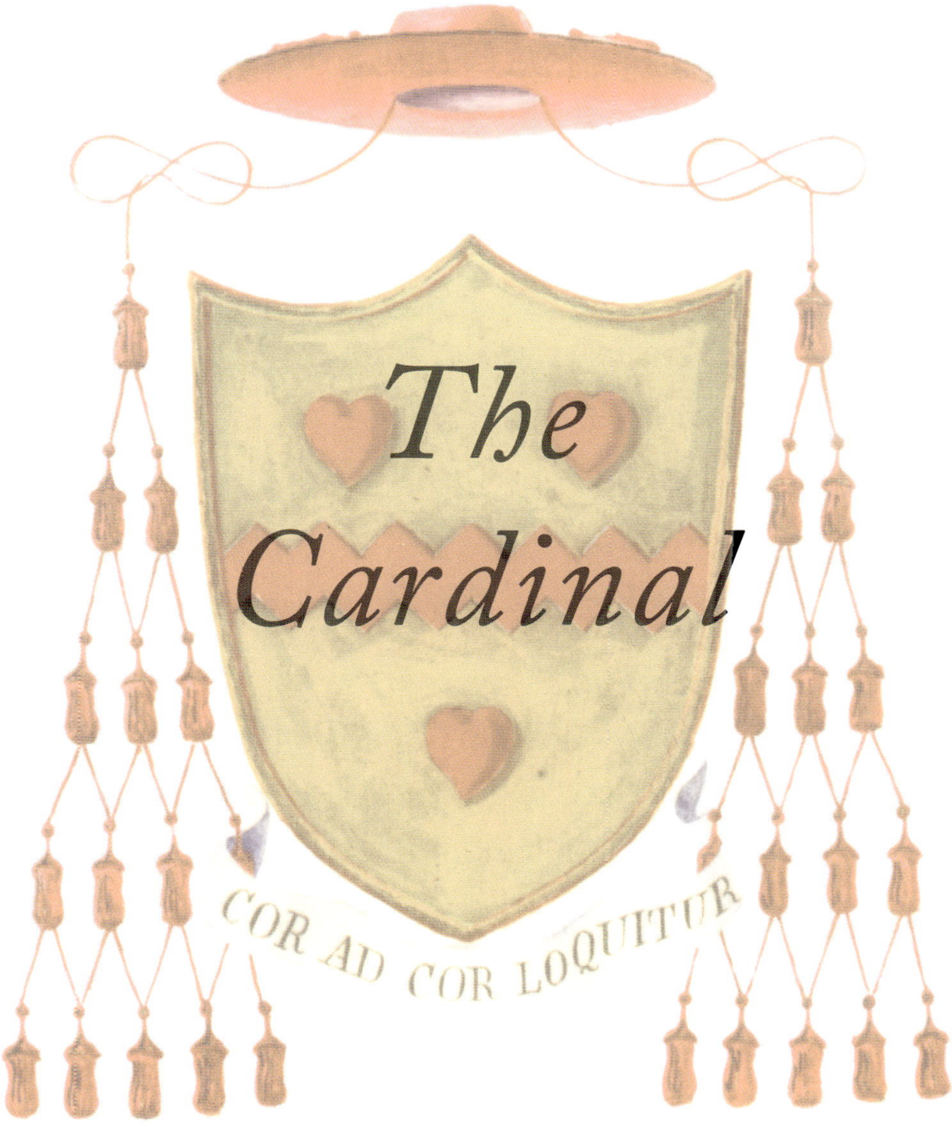

Chapter 6

The Cardinal

(1879-1890)

JOHN HENRY NEWMAN was created Cardinal of the Catholic Church by Pope Leo XIII on 12 May 1879 and he acknowledged the *biglietto* sent by the Pope with his famous *Biglietto Speech.* His stay in Rome was marred by a very bad cold, which kept him confined to his room much of the time, unable even to go to Mass on St Philip's Day. The doctors ordered fresh sea air and sunshine in Livorno, on his way back to England, but he had a relapse on the Ligurian Coast and was again confined to his room. He returned in a weakened state to a joyous welcome at the Oratory in Birmingham on 1 July.

After all the excitement about his cardinalate had died down, his life assumed a peaceful routine with intermittent visits to Oxford, London, and even a holiday in Wales. His health was generally good, but he suffered from weakness and fits of sleepiness, as he called them, then eventually from failing eyesight, deafness and loss of feeling in his fingertips, which made writing nearly impossible. He tended to fall down rather easily and two falls at the beginning of 1880 cost him three broken ribs. His preaching days, too, gradually came to an end.

He was not inactive, however. He still kept up a large correspondence, though he had to dictate much of it. He had visitors from time to time, but found that he had to decline most invitations to make visits or appearances himself. The last volumes of the uniform edition of his works, the two volumes of *Select Treatises of St Athanasius*, were published in February 1881 (he was to revise these again in 1887).

His last years were calm and peaceful, though still with an occasional controversy. He did not allow falsehood or mistaken belief to go unchallenged. He kept his sense of humour, laughing at times at his own age and weakness. Those who visited him spoke most often and movingly of his simple and deep humility. Lord Coleridge described him as being "simple and humble and playful as a child", and Frederick Bowles exclaimed after a visit from him, "what humility, what charity, what loving condescension" (M. Trevor, *Light in Winter*, pp. 628, 635). In March 1885, Newman visited his friend, Dean Church, who found Newman's "old smile and twinkle of the eye" still there (LD XXXI, 128, FN 4). That same year he was photographed by Barraud in his London studio. The well-known photographer was unable to get just the look he wanted until Fr Neville began to speak to Newman of the zoo which they had visited. Talk of the animals, in which he had always had a great interest, enlivened Newman and the photographer got his desired shot.

The poet, Francis Turner Palgrave, was granted an interview with the Cardinal at the Oratory in 1886. As was to be expected, he found him much changed since he had seen him many years before. His voice, which he knew from hearing him in Littlemore, still had "much of its old strange sweetness", however, though "the look of almost anxious searching had passed into the look of perfect peace" (*LD* XXXI, 184, FN 5).

Peace was, in fact, the distinguishing mark of Newman's last years. His was a peace from within: his resignation to God's will, which he had long cultivated, had become a waiting in quiet expectation to see Him face to face. Nearly all his friends died before he did; of his own immediate family only his brother Frank outlived him. He had long prepared himself for death; he was ready.

On 9 August 1890 Newman received a visit from his niece, Grace, the only daughter of his sister, Harriett, who had ceased to have contact with Newman even before his conversion. Newman had seen Grace just once when she was three years old. She had visited Littlemore with her mother at that time. Her visit to the Oratory that summer day was the healing of a division in the family, which must have pleased Newman very much. That night Newman took ill with pneumonia. He declined rapidly, received extreme unction, and died on 11 August at 8:45 in the evening.

The event was in all the papers the next day. They praised his integrity, his honesty, his purity of intention and his gentleness. The funeral Mass was in the Oratory Church on 19 August and he was buried in the Oratory cemetery at Rednal, in the grave of Ambrose

St John, as was his explicit wish. His memorial plaque in the Oratory cloisters reads: *Ex umbris et imaginibus in veritatem* – out of shadows and images into the truth.

I have this very day learned that the offer of a Cardinal's Hat is to be made to me with the privilege of living still here as before. So great a kindness, made with so personal a feeling towards me by the Pope, I could not resist, and I shall accept it. It puts an end to all those reports that my teaching is not Catholic or my books trustworthy, which has been so great a trial to me so long.

LD XXIX, 50, Letter to Anne Mozley, 1 March 1879.

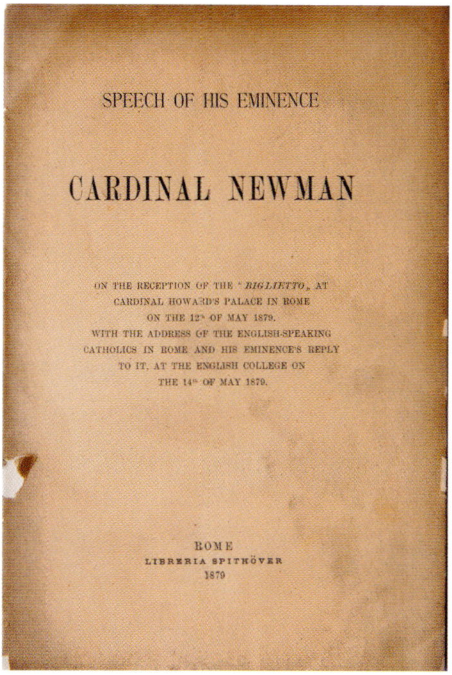

SPEECH OF HIS EMINENCE

CARDINAL NEWMAN

ON THE RECEPTION OF THE "*BIGLIETTO*" AT CARDINAL HOWARD'S PALACE IN ROME ON THE 12th OF MAY 1879. WITH THE ADDRESS OF THE ENGLISH-SPEAKING CATHOLICS IN ROME AND HIS EMINENCE'S REPLY TO IT, AT THE ENGLISH COLLEGE ON THE 14th OF MAY 1879.

ROME
LIBRERIA SPITHÖVER
1879

Liberalism in religion is the doctrine that there is no positive truth in religion, but that one creed is as good as another.... It is inconsistent with any recognition of any religion, as *true*. It teaches that all are to be tolerated, for all are matters of opinion.

Addresses, 64, Biglietto Speech.

It was a beautiful speech, quite the old John Henry Newman speaking out the truth, yet not wounding a single heart.

LD XXIX, 144, FN 1, Letter of E. B. Pusey to the Revd Father Belaney, 20 May 1879.

Cardinal Newman's study

Newman wrote from Rome to a fellow Oratorian:
It is useless to think of preparing *my* rooms. Two days before I return they may be swept out – but I must ask the Fathers to let me rent the one next to my own, (…) and I must have an altar there. …

LD XXIX, 131, Letter to John Norris, 27 May 1879.

…Then I must have endless wardrobes for my vestments, and for robes, which I shall never wear. I almost think I shall be dead before I am to rights. My tailor's bill will be £200!

LD XXIX, 131, Letter to John Norris, 27 May 1879.

In Rome, 1879. From the right: Fr Pope, Fr Neville (standing), Fr Eagleton, Cardinal Newman, the Cardinal's Gentiluomo, the Cardinal's Cautatorio or train bearer

Praise to the Holiest in the height,
And in the depth be praise:
In all His words most wonderful;
Most sure in all His ways!

VV, 353, The Dream of Gerontius.

And now I will ask you, my dear friends, to pray for me, that I may be as the presence of the Holy Father amongst you....

Addresses, 105, Address in the Oratory Church upon returning to Birmingham from Rome, 1 July 1879.

Bishop Ullathorne wrote to Newman upon his return to England:
The Pope's words have been completely realized. He wished to do an act pleasing to the Catholics of England, and to England itself, and that pleasure has been given in full measure.

LD XXIX, 148, FN 1, Letter from Bishop Ullathorne, 2 July 1879.

Simply to His grace and wholly
  Light and life and strength belong,
And I love, supremely, solely,
  Him the holy, Him the strong.

VV, 327, The Dream of Gerontius

After his return to England from Rome, Cardinal Newman wrote to a friend:
I got here yesterday, and am still very weak. I am not allowed to exert myself in any way for three weeks, when I suppose I shall go to London to receive Addresses, etc. Is it not very wonderful? I keep saying to myself, what is left for me but to die?

LD XXIX, 146, Letter to Lord Coleridge, 2 July 1879.

And I take with joy whatever
  Now besets me, pain or fear,
And with a strong will I sever
  All the ties which bind me here.

VV, 327, The Dream of Gerontius.

The last message I had about my promotion was a few days ago from a working man, unknown to the friend who met him as she was coming out of a London church. 'Are you a Catholic? Is this Cardinal Newman's church? Do you know him? Tell him the workmen of England are rejoiced to know that the Pope has done so good a deed as to make him a Cardinal.' It is so wonderful a change as to cow one.

LD XXIX, Letter to T. W. Allies, 23 November 1879.

Adoration aye be given,
With and through the angelic host,
To the God of earth and heaven,
Father, Son and Holy Ghost.

VV, 328, The Dream of Gerontius

Memorial plaque of John and Jemima Mozley

I have just heard the tidings of my Sister's death. She died some minutes before noon to-day. Not with her on my mind, I was saying to myself a day or two ago, 'I have not yet had a friend die on Christmas Day'.

LD XXIX, 215, Letter to Lord Blachford, Christmas Day, 1879.

Bust of Cardinal Newman, Trinity College Garden

Newman visited Trinity College, Oxford, 22-25 May 1880

It was one of the great moments of my life. The Cardinal, a wan little old man with a shrivelled face and a large nose, and one of the most beautiful expressions which ever appeared on a human being, talked to me for a couple of hours, prostrating me with his exquisite modesty. He wanted to know if the snapdragons, to which he had written a poem, still grew on the wall between Trinity and Balliol….

LD XXIX, 430, Appendix 3, quoted from Douglas Sladen, My Long Life, *London 1939, 46–47.*

George Gilbert Scott was the great great grandson of Thomas Scott, whose writings so influenced Newman when he young. He had become a Catholic in 1880 and is said to have lost much of his architectural practice as a result. Cardinal Newman wrote to him:
We want a design in tile or alabaster or both for an apse [for St Philip's chapel]. Before troubling you with any details, may I ask whether it falls within your profession to aid us in this matter. We have very little means of meeting what may be more expensive than we fancy – but we propose to do first one portion, then another, as we are prospered.

LD XXIX, 286, Letter to George Gilbert Scott, 3 July 1880.

The Chapel of St Philip Neri in the Oratory Church, Birmingham

Cardinal Newman continued to help those who were in doubt concerning religion:
Now then, if God has given us so great a blessing, as 'a pillar and ground of the truth,' and told us to join all of us in 'the Apostles' fellowship', how can I, in gratitude, how can I in love to the souls of men, be content to let them, to let you, be as sheep without a Shepherd, and hold communion with you, as you are, as if God did not call you to come to the Spiritual Home which He has provided for you? that is to the Catholic Church. The good Samaritan sent on the wounded man – but I should be like the Priest and Levite, passing by on the other side, if I kept silence, and said nothing to you about the Home and the Hospital which our Good Lord has provided for all for whom He has shed His precious blood.

LD XXIX, Letter to an Unknown Correspondent, 25 July 1880.

Cardinal Newman – wax portrait, 1990

A Cardinal has of all things nearest to his heart the well-being of Holy Church, and how can I have a greater consolation and encouragement in my last years, than in your persons to be reminded, by the distance between us, of her expanse of territory – by your zeal on her behalf, of her life and strength – and by your youth, of the promise of her future. May her glorious future and the career of every one of you be bound together by an indissoluble tie, to the prosperity and peace of both Mother and children!

LD XXIX, 292, Letter to the Catholic Young Men's National Union, U.S.A., August 1880.

Cardinal Newman's study, the Birmingham Oratory – photograph, c. *1958*

Newman wrote to the son of a friend who had dislocated his knee. He enclosed a present:

The ring which accompanies this note is a present made to me near 30 years ago by the Catholics of Calefornia [sic]. It is made of pure Calefornian [sic] gold. The great mass of it, in the shape of a heart, is as it was picked up in the diggings. I find it rather too large and heavy. I wonder whether it will fit you. Can you construe the Latin?

LD XXIX, 308, Letter to Clement Hungerford Pollen, 26 October 1880.

Newman preached in the London Oratory church on Sunday 26 June, 1881 and received the following reaction from a member of the congregation:

I hope your Eminence will allow me to express the immense pleasure and admiration with which I glowed in hearing your Sermon on Sunday. I will not dwell on its wonderful simplicity in combination with its keen logical power, but I can truly say that I never heard any thing more truly Catholic in my life.... Every Christian of every denomination – if he believed only in the Lord Jesus and His word – might have heard it with perfect satisfaction.

LD XXIX, 386, FN 1, Letter from Bonamy Price, 29 June 1881.

Cardinal Newman memorial, the London Oratory

Fr Henry Lewis Bellasis, CO, and Cardinal Newman

In December 1883 Newman heard that Mark Pattison was in his last illness. Pattison had been a Tractarian and had shared his religious views, but had then drifted away in the opposite direction. Fr. Neville, Newman's secretary, wrote of the episode:

The Cardinal was rather seriously ill in bed with bronchitis when this sad news came, but, at once he determined to do what he felt would be best – to go himself to the sick man. The doctors gave their forebodings of what would be the result to himself if he went, but he would not be deterred. "Is the little life left me," he said, "to be weighed against the chance of good in a case such as this? Let the doctors say what they will, I shall go!"

LD XXX, 288, FN 3.

Thou dost bring me on year by year, by Thy wonderful Providence, from youth to age, with the most perfect wisdom, and with the most perfect love.

MD, 522.

Newman was sent a copy of The Dream of Gerontius *which had belonged to General Gordon and in which he had made notes. He writes of it to a friend:*
I will but say a word about Gordon. What struck me so much in his use of 'The Dream etc' was that in St Paul's words he 'died daily' – he was always on his death bed, fulfilling the common advice that we should ever pass the day, as if it was to be our last.

LD XXXI, 67, Letter to Lord Blachford, 19 May 1885.

Rouse thee, my fainting soul, and play the man;
 And through such waning span
Of life and thought as still has to be trod,
 Prepare to meet thy God

VV, 325, The Dream of Gerontius.

Bishop William Ullathorne, Bishop of Birmingham 1850–1888

Bishop Ullathorne wrote to a friend about a visit he made to Cardinal Newman on 18 August 1887:

We had a long and cheery talk, but as I was rising to leave an action of his caused a scene I shall never forget. … He said in low and humble accents, "My dear Lord, will you do me a great favour?" "What is it?" I asked. He glided down on his knees, bent down his venerable head, and said, "Give me your blessing." What could I do with him before me in such a posture? … So I laid my hand on his head and said: "My dear Lord Cardinal, notwithstanding all laws to the contrary, I pray God to bless you, and that His Holy Spirit may be full in your heart."

Ward II, 531.

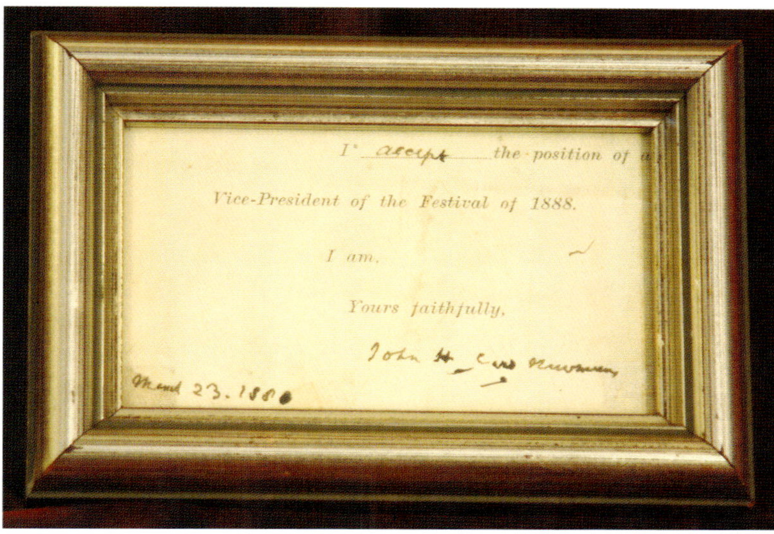
I accept the position of a
Vice-President of the Festival of 1888.
I am,
Yours faithfully,
John H. Card. Newman
March 23. 1888

Newman attended the Birmingham Music Festival 28-31 August 1888

Music … is the expression of ideas greater and more profound than any in the visible world, ideas, which centre indeed in Him whom Catholicism manifests, who is the seat of all beauty, order and perfection whatever, still ideas after all which are not those on which Revelation directly and principally fixes our gaze.

Idea, 80.

Cardinal Newman said his last Mass on Christmas Day 1889. Fr Neville relates:

Cardinal Newman's private chapel, Birmingham Oratory

...after which Feast he always declined to say Mass himself from fear of an accident. ... Reverence forbade such a risk. Nevertheless he learnt by heart a Mass of the Blessed Virgin and a Mass of the Dead. One or other of these Masses he repeated daily, whole or part, and with the due ceremonies, for the chance that he hoped for, since his sight and strength varied, that with the brighter sunlight of the spring he might some day find himself in condition to say Mass once again. He was determined, he said, that no want of readiness on his part should cause him to miss the opportunity should it occur. This preparation became to him the great pleasure of the day, both from what he could look forward to in hope, and also from the reverence that filled him by the solemnity of the words and different actions.

Ward II, 532-533.

"I declare, to me," he said, and he clasped his hands on his knees, and looked forward as if soliloquizing, – "to me nothing is so consoling, so piercing, so thrilling, so overcoming, as the Mass, said as it is among us. I could attend Masses for ever, and not be tired. It is not a mere form of words, – it is a great action, the greatest action that can be on earth. It is, not the invocation merely, but, if I dare use the word, the evocation of the Eternal."

LG, 327-328.

Cardinal Newman's Titular Church: San Giorgio in Velabro, Rome

So long Thy power hath blessed me, sure it still
Will lead me on,
O'er moor and fen, o'er crag and torrent, till
The night is gone;
And with the morn those angel faces smile
Which I have loved long since, and lost awhile.

VV, 157, The Pillar of the Cloud

Fr Neville wrote of the Cardinal's entrance into his room the evening of 9 August 1890, two days before his death:

...[H]is footstep was slow yet firm and elastic; ... soon when seen, his bearing was in keeping with his step; – unbent, erect to the full height of his best days in the 'fifties; he was without support of any kind. His whole carriage was, it may be said, soldier-like, and so dignified; and his countenance was most attractive to look at; even great age seemed to have gone from his face, and with it all careworn signs; his very look conveyed the cheerfulness and gratitude of his mind....

Ward II, 537.

Cardinal Newman, from his last photographic sitting c. *1890*

Proficiscere, anima Christiana, de hoc mundo!
Go forth upon thy journey, Christian soul!
Go from this world! Go, in the name of God
The Omnipotent Father, who created thee!
Go, in the name of Jesus Christ, our Lord,
Son of the living God, who bled for thee!
Go, in the name of the Holy Spirit, who
Hath been poured out on thee!

VV, 330–331, The Dream of Gerontius

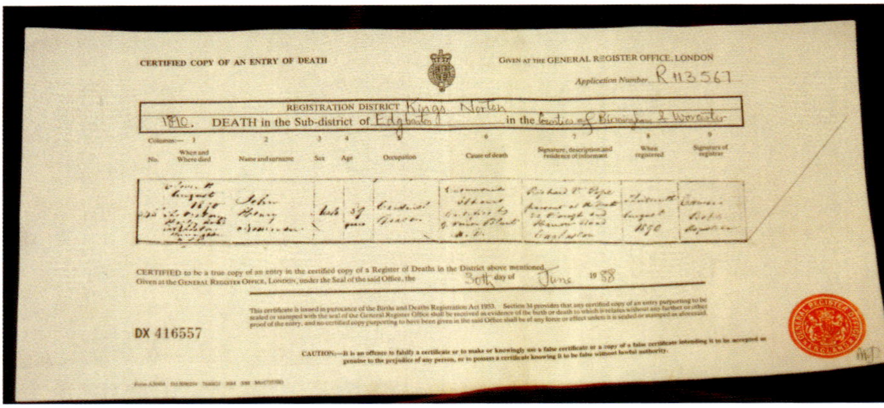
CERTIFIED COPY OF AN ENTRY OF DEATH

GIVEN AT THE GENERAL REGISTER OFFICE, LONDON

Application Number R113567

REGISTRATION DISTRICT Kings Norton

1890. DEATH in the Sub-district of Edgbaston in the Counties of Birmingham & Worcester

No.	When and Where died	Name and surname	Sex	Age	Occupation	Cause of death	Signature, description and residence of informant	When registered	Signature of registrar
	11th August 1890	John Henry Newman	Male	89 years	Cardinal Deacon		Richard V. Pope	Thirteenth August 1890	

CERTIFIED to be a true copy of an entry in the certified copy of a Register of Deaths in the District above mentioned. Given at the GENERAL REGISTER OFFICE, LONDON, under the Seal of the said Office, the 30th day of June 1988

DX 416557

Copy of the death certificate of John Henry Cardinal Newman

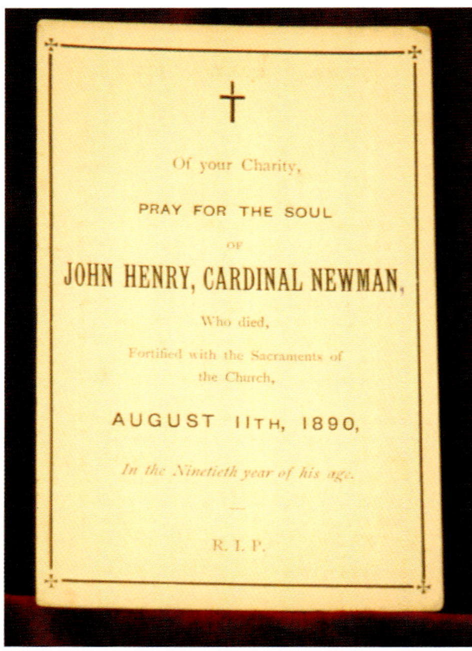
Of your Charity,

PRAY FOR THE SOUL

OF

JOHN HENRY, CARDINAL NEWMAN,

Who died,

Fortified with the Sacraments of the Church,

AUGUST 11TH, 1890,

In the Ninetieth year of his age.

R. I. P.

Memorial Card

By the death of Cardinal NEWMAN the Church of Rome loses one of its two great English Cardinals, the literature of England loses one of its great masters, and the world loses one of the chiefest of its saints.

Pall Mall Gazette, *14 August 1890, as quoted in Positio, 410.*

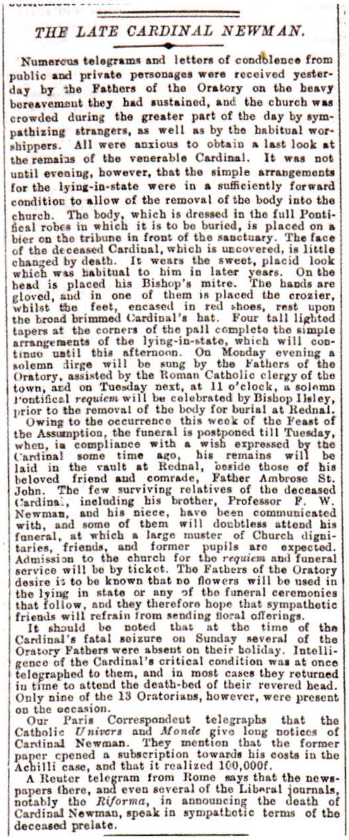

THE LATE CARDINAL NEWMAN.

Numerous telegrams and letters of condolence from public and private personages were received yesterday by the Fathers of the Oratory on the heavy bereavement they had sustained, and the church was crowded during the greater part of the day by sympathizing strangers, as well as by the habitual worshippers. All were anxious to obtain a last look at the remains of the venerable Cardinal. It was not until evening, however, that the simple arrangements for the lying-in-state were in a sufficiently forward condition to allow of the removal of the body into the church. The body, which is dressed in the full Pontifical robes in which it is to be buried, is placed on a bier on the tribune in front of the sanctuary. The face of the deceased Cardinal, which is uncovered, is little changed by death. It wears the sweet, placid look which was habitual to him in later years. On the head is placed his Bishop's mitre. The hands are gloved, and in one of them is placed the crozier, whilst the feet, encased in red shoes, rest upon the broad brimmed Cardinal's hat. Four tall lighted tapers at the corners of the pall complete the simple arrangements of the lying-in-state, which will continue until this afternoon. On Monday evening a solemn dirge will be sung by the Fathers of the Oratory, assisted by the Roman Catholic clergy of the town, and on Tuesday next, at 11 o'clock, a solemn Pontifical *requiem* will be celebrated by Bishop Ilsley, prior to the removal of the body for burial at Rednal.

Owing to the occurrence this week of the Feast of the Assumption, the funeral is postponed till Tuesday, when, in compliance with a wish expressed by the Cardinal some time ago, his remains will be laid in the vault at Rednal, beside those of his beloved friend and comrade, Father Ambrose St. John. The few surviving relatives of the deceased Cardinal, including his brother, Professor F. W. Newman, and his niece, have been communicated with, and some of them will doubtless attend his funeral, at which a large muster of Church dignitaries, friends, and former pupils are expected. Admission to the church for the *requiem* and funeral service will be by ticket. The Fathers of the Oratory desire it to be known that no flowers will be used in the lying in state or any of the funeral ceremonies that follow, and they therefore hope that sympathetic friends will refrain from sending floral offerings.

It should be noted that at the time of the Cardinal's fatal seizure on Sunday several of the Oratory Fathers were absent on their holiday. Intelligence of the Cardinal's critical condition was at once telegraphed to them, and in most cases they returned in time to attend the death-bed of their revered head. Only nine of the 13 Oratorians, however, were present on the occasion.

Our Paris Correspondent telegraphs that the Catholic *Univers* and *Monde* give long notices of Cardinal Newman. They mention that the former paper opened a subscription towards his costs in the Achilli case, and that it realized 100,000f.

A Reuter telegram from Rome says that the newspapers there, and even several of the Liberal journals, notably the *Riforma*, in announcing the death of Cardinal Newman, speak in sympathetic terms of the deceased prelate.

The Times, *13 August 1890.*

Of one thing we may be sure, that the memory of his pure and noble life, untouched by worldliness, unsoured by any trace of fanaticism, will endure, and that whether Rome canonizes him or not he will be canonized in the thoughts of pious people of many creeds in England. The saint and the poet in him will survive.

Leading Article The Times, *12 August 1890.*

Report of the death of Cardinal Newman, The Times, *12 August 1890*

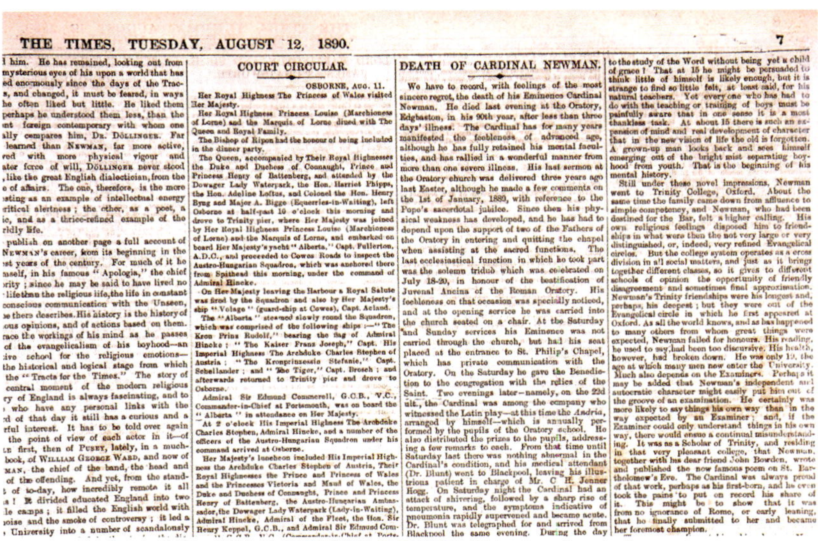

THE TIMES, TUESDAY, AUGUST 12, 1890. 7

l him. He has remained, looking out from mysterious eyes of his upon a world that has ed enormously since the days of the Tracs, and changed, it must be feared, in ways he often liked but little. He liked them perhaps he understood them less, than the nt foreign contemporary with whom one ally compares him, DR. DÖLLINGER. Far learned than NEWMAN, far more active, red with more physical vigour and ater force of will, DÖLLINGER never stood , like the great English dialectician, from the e of affairs. The one, therefore, is the more sting as an example of intellectual energy ritical alertness; the other, as a poet, a ic, and as a thrice-refined example of the rldly life.

publish on another page a full account of NEWMAN's career, from its beginning in the st years of the century. For much of it he mself, in his famous "Apologia," the chief rity; since he may be said to have lived no life than the religious life, the life in constant conscious communication with the Unseen, e there describes. His history is the history of ous opinions, and of actions based on them. race the workings of his mind as he passes of the evangelicalism of his boyhood—an ive school for the religious emotions— the historical and logical stage from which the "Tracts for the Times." The story of central moment of the modern religious ry of England is always fascinating, and to who have any personal links with the d of that day it still has a curious and a rful interest. It has to be told over again the point of view of each actor in it—of n first, then of PUSEY, lately, in a much- book, of WILLIAM GEORGE WARD, and now of MAN, the chief of the band, the head and of the offending. And yet, from the stand- of to-day, how incredibly remote it all s! It divided educated England into two le camps; it filled the English world with oise and the smoke of controversy; it led a University into a number of scandalously

COURT CIRCULAR.

OSBORNE, AUG. 11.

Her Royal Highness The Princess of Wales visited Her Majesty.

Her Royal Highness Princess Louise (Marchioness of Lorne) and the Marquis of Lorne dined with The Queen and Royal Family.

The Bishop of Ripon had the honour of being included in the dinner party.

The Queen, accompanied by Their Royal Highnesses the Duke and Duchess of Connaught, Prince and Princess Henry of Battenberg, and attended by the Dowager Lady Waterpark, the Hon. Harriet Phipps, the Hon. Adeline Loftus, and Colonel the Hon. Henry Byng and Major A. Bigge (Equerries-in-Waiting), left Osborne at half-past 10 o'clock this morning and drove to Trinity pier, where Her Majesty was joined by Her Royal Highness Princess Louise (Marchioness of Lorne) and the Marquis of Lorne, and embarked on board Her Majesty's yacht "Alberta," Capt. Fullerton, A.D.C., and proceeded to Cowes Roads to inspect the Austro-Hungarian Squadron, which was anchored there from Spithead this morning, under the command of Admiral Hincke.

On Her Majesty leaving the Harbour a Royal Salute was fired by the Squadron and also by Her Majesty's ship "Volage" (guard-ship at Cowes), Capt. Acland.

The "Alberta" steamed slowly round the Squadron, which was comprised of the following ships:—"The Kron Prinz Rudolf," bearing the flag of Admiral Hincke; "The Kaiser Franz Joseph," Capt. His Imperial Highness The Archduke Charles Stephen of Austria; "The Kronprinzessin Stefanie," Capt. Schellander; and "The Tiger," Capt. Brosch; and afterwards returned to Trinity pier and drove to Osborne.

Admiral Sir Edmund Commerell, G.C.B., V.C., Commander-in-Chief at Portsmouth, was on board the "Alberta" in attendance on Her Majesty.

At 2 o'clock His Imperial Highness The Archduke Charles Stephen, Admiral Hincke, and a number of the officers of the Austro-Hungarian Squadron under his command arrived at Osborne.

Her Majesty's luncheon included His Imperial Highness the Archduke Charles Stephen of Austria, Their Royal Highnesses the Prince and Princess of Wales and the Princesses Victoria and Maud of Wales, the Duke and Duchess of Connaught, Prince and Princess Henry of Battenberg, the Austro-Hungarian Ambassador, the Dowager Lady Waterpark (Lady-in-Waiting), Admiral Hincke, Admiral of the Fleet, the Hon. Sir Henry Keppel, G.C.B., and Admiral Sir Edmund Com-

DEATH OF CARDINAL NEWMAN.

We have to record, with feelings of the most sincere regret, the death of his Eminence Cardinal Newman. He died last evening at the Oratory, Edgbaston, in his 90th year, after less than three days' illness. The Cardinal has for many years manifested the feebleness of advanced age, although he has fully retained his mental faculties, and has rallied in a wonderful manner from more than one severe illness. His last sermon at the Oratory church was delivered three years ago last Easter, although he made a few comments on the 1st of January, 1889, with reference to the Pope's sacerdotal jubilee. Since then his physical weakness has developed, and he has had to depend upon the support of two of the Fathers of the Oratory in entering and quitting the chapel when assisting at the sacred functions. The last ecclesiastical function in which he took part was the solemn triduo which was celebrated on July 18-20, in honour of the beatification of Juvenal Ancina of the Roman Oratory. His feebleness on that occasion was specially noticed, and at the opening service he was carried into the church seated on a chair. At the Saturday and Sunday services his Eminence was not carried through the church, but had his seat placed at the entrance to St. Philip's Chapel, which has private communication with the Oratory. On the Saturday he gave the Benediction to the congregation with the relics of the Saint. Two evenings later—namely, on the 22d ult., the Cardinal was among the company who witnessed the Latin play—at this time the *Andria*, arranged by himself—which is annually performed by the pupils of the Oratory school. He also distributed the prizes to the pupils, addressing a few remarks to each. From that time until Saturday last there was nothing abnormal in the Cardinal's condition, and his medical attendant (Dr. Blunt) went to Blackpool, leaving his illustrious patient in charge of Mr. C. H. Jenner Hogg. On Saturday night the Cardinal had an attack of shivering, followed by a sharp rise of temperature, and the symptoms indicative of pneumonia rapidly supervened and became acute. Dr. Blunt was telegraphed for and arrived from Blackpool the same evening. During the day

to the study of the Word without being yet a child of grace? That at 15 he might be persuaded to think little of himself is likely enough, but it is strange to find so little felt, at least said, for his natural teachers. Yet every one who has had to do with the teaching or training of boys must be painfully aware that in one sense it is a most thankless task. At about 15 there is such an expansion of mind and real development of character that in the new vision of life the old is forgotten. A grown-up man looks back and sees himself emerging out of the bright mist separating boyhood from youth. That is the beginning of his mental history.

Still under these novel impressions, Newman went to Trinity College, Oxford. About the same time the family came down from affluence to simple competency, and Newman, who had been destined for the Bar, felt a higher calling. His own religious feelings disposed him to friendships in what were then the not very large or very distinguished, or, indeed, very refined Evangelical circles. But the college system operates as a cross division in all social matters, and just as it brings together different classes, so it gives to different schools of opinion the opportunity of friendly disagreement and sometimes final approximation. Newman's Trinity friendships were his longest and, perhaps, his deepest; but they were out of the Evangelical circle in which he first appeared at Oxford. As all the world knows, and as has happened to many others from whom great things were expected, Newman failed for honours. His reading, he used to say, had been too discursive. His health, however, had broken down. He was only 19, the age at which many men now enter the University. Much also depends on the Examiners. Perhaps it may be added that Newman's independent and autocratic character might easily put him out of the groove of an examination. He certainly was more likely to say things his own way than in the way expected by an Examiner; and, if the Examiner could only understand things in his own way, there would ensue a continual misunderstanding. It was as a Scholar of Trinity, and residing in that very pleasant college, that Newman, together with his dear friend John Bowden, wrote and published the now famous poem on St. Bartholomew's Eve. The Cardinal was always proud of that work, perhaps as his first-born, and he even took the pains to put on record his share of it. This might be to show that it was from no ignorance of Rome, or early leaning, that he finally submitted to her and became her foremost champion.

Gravestone of John Henry Cardinal Newman and Ambrose St John, Rednal – photograph by Elke Deimel

I know, O my God, I must change, if I am to see Thy face! I must undergo the change of death. Body and soul must die to this world. … None but the holy can see Thee.

MD, 508.

Epilogue: Littlemore since Newman

Epilogue

The College after Newman

The Newman collection at The College has helped us to look at Bl. John Henry Newman's life, a life lived to the full. At the end of this portrait let us look into the history of the place where the pictures and memorabilia are found today.

When John Henry Newman left The College in February 1846, his friend, Charles Marriott, who had taken over the lease, installed a printing press and produced some books in the following two years. The work being too hard on his health, he then left the building to the Diocese of Oxford. It became almshouses administered by the Vicars of Littlemore for just a hundred years. In 1936, on the occasion of the centenary of the Church of St Mary and St Nicholas, built by Newman at Littlemore, a plaque commemorating Newman's presence there was placed on the outside wall of The College.

In the early 1950s the Fathers of the Birmingham Oratory acquired the building. It was falling into ruin and they undertook a complete renovation at considerable cost. With the help of drawings by Newman and his friends, the historically important rooms could be identified and restored to their original appearance: Newman's bedroom, which had served as a study as well, the small oratory, and the large hall where he had placed his library. Even the garden was replanted in Victorian style and contributes greatly to the atmosphere of The College. On 27 May 1960 the then Archbishop of Birmingham, Francis Grimshaw, celebrated the first Mass in the restored oratory. It was this same Archbishop who had introduced the diocesan Process of Newman's Beatification in 1958.

The Oratorian Fathers also renovated the old rooms in the almshouses without interfering with the outward appearance of The College. For more than twenty years the families who rented the five remaining cottages at The College showed visitors the Newman rooms. Certain Newman Friends still remember that Mrs Clarke, an Anglican, who was well on in years and who had brought up her family at The College, spoke with fervour about "her Cardinal". From 1982 to 1986 Miss Patricia Taylor devotedly looked after The College as its curator and set up a small Newman museum in the former library containing a well documented collection of engravings and modern prints of paintings, some photographs, a few books, among them two first editions, and some Newman memorabilia given to The College by the Birmingham Oratory or collected by Miss Taylor. In the meantime The College was given listed building status by the government.

In 1987 the everyday care of The College was entrusted by the Birmingham Oratory to The Spiritual Family The Work and its International Center of Newman Friends. The purchase of Ambrose Cottage next to The College has enabled more members of the Community to reside at Littlemore and not only to maintain but to build-up The College as a place of prayer, pilgrimage, retreat and study in the spirit of Newman and in the spirit of the charism of The Work. In 1997 The Work leased The College from the Birmingham Oratory and is now responsible in great part for its upkeep both financially and practically.

Each year visitors from all over the world come to The College to pay tribute to and learn more about Bl. John Henry Cardinal Newman. The library is generally the starting point of a guided tour of The College. The tour also includes Newman's room and the chapel where the Blessed Sacrament has been reserved since 1990. In addition, visitors may visit Newman's church and see the school, built while he was at Littlemore. There are cottages available for guests who wish to spend some days in study or retreat at The College. They can join the community in their prayer in Newman's chapel.

Newman wrote in his *Apologia Pro Vita Sua*, "as I made Littlemore a place of retirement for myself, so did I offer it to others" (*Apo.*, 160). In this spirit, The College offers an atmosphere conducive to reflection and prayer, study and fellowship also today, and the Spiritual Family The Work is happy to welcome anyone who wants to experience something of the peace and sanctity which Newman's presence has imprinted on this place. For more information visit: www.newmanfriendsinternational.org.

List of Illustrations

1.1	Plaque on London Stock Exchange; photograph	*page* 10
1.2	The Foudrinier Family; photograph of painting by John Downman, original in National Portrait Gallery	11
1.3	Collage of the Newman Family	11
1.4	Greycourt House at Ham; photograph by Elke Deimel	12
1.5	17 Southampton Place; photograph by Elke Deimel	12
1.6	Newman's first letter home from school; copy of original in Birmingham Oratory	13
1.7	Great Ealing School; copy of engraving	14
1.8	Church of St Mary, Ealing; copy of engraving	14
1.9	Revd Thomas Scott; engraving by J. Le Conte	15
2.1	Trinity College; engraving, coloured, by J. Le Keux, 1835	21
2.2	John William Bowden; painting	21
2.2	Trinity College; engraving by J. Le Keux, 1835	22
2.3	Trinity College; painting by Elo Alike-Schuenmeann, *c.* 2000	22
2.4	Trinity College; photograph by Elke Deimel	23
2.5	Trinity College; engraving by J. Shelton	23
2.6	Crest of Trinity College	24
2.7	Newman's Viola; photograph by kind permission of the Birmingham Oratory	25
2.8	Newman's "Obiettamento"; photograph by kind permission of the Birmingham Oratory	25
3.1	Oriel College; engraving by J. Le Keux, 1822	32
3.2	Oriel College, the front quadrangle; engraving by J. Le Keux, 1834	32
3.3	John Keble; engraving from a portrait by Richmond	33
3.4	E. B. Pusey; engraving	33
3.5	John Henry Newman; lithograph by J.A. Vinter, 1850 after the painting by Maria Giberne	34
3.6	Old St Clement's Church at the Plain, Oxford; colour print from engraving	34
3.7	Over Worton Church; from a postcard	35
3.8	New St Clement's Church; engraving by J. Le Keux, 1836	35

3.9 St Alban Hall, Oxford; engraving by J. & H.S. Storer, 1822 36
3.10 Oriel College; engraving by Emery Walker, 1915–18 36
3.11 Richard Hurrell Froude; courtesy of Oriel College 37
3.12 Froude's *Remains*; photograph of title page 37
3.13 Maria Rosina Giberne, an early self-portrait 38
3.14 Mary Newman; sketch by Maria Giberne, *c.* 1827 38
3.15 Henry Wilberforce 39
3.16 Book given by Newman to his Godson, John William Wilberforce; photograph of title page 39
3.17 University Church of St Mary the Virgin; engraving by J. Le Keux, 1833 40
3.18 The pulpit of St Mary the Virgin; photograph by Elke Deimel 41
3.19 John Henry Newman, preaching; engraving, 1841 41
3.20 A view in Sicily; steel engraving, hand coloured 42
3.21 Leonforte, Sicily; postcard view 42
3.22 Lead, Kindly Light, in Newman's handwriting 43
3.23 The spire of the University Church of St Mary the Virgin; engraving, by J. & H.S. Storer, 1822 44
3. 24 John Henry Newman, Vicar of St Mary the Virgin; detail of am ink sketch *c.* 1841 44
3.25 John Henry Newman; large-scale pencil sketch by Anthony Stones 45
3.26 Oriel College; copperplate engraving, by David Loggan from *Oxonia Illustrata*, 1675 46
3.27 The Newman window at Oriel College (design by Vivienne Haig, realisation by Douglas Hogg), detail 47
3.28 Crest of Oriel College 47
3.29 John Henry Newman; engraving after bust by Richard Westmacott, 1841 48
3.30 John Henry Newman; postcard of water-colour portrait by Sir William Ross, 1845. By kind permission of the Warden and Fellows of Keble College, Oxford 48
3.31 Rose Mount, Rose Hill; photograph by Elke Deimel 49
3.32 Rose Bank, now called Grove House; photograph by Elke Deimel 49

3.33 Thomas Mozley; sketch by Maria Giberne, 1832 50
3.34 Harriet Newman; detail of sketch of the Newman Family by Maria Giberne 50
3.35 The Church of St Mary and St Nicholas, Littlemore; engraving from Ingram's *Memorials of Oxford*, 1837 51
3.36. Memorial to Newman's mother; photograph by Elke Deimel 51
3.37 The Church of St Mary and St Nicholas and adjacent school; engraving by W.A. Delamotte 52
3.38 J.R. Bloxam 52
3.39 The Littlemore schoolhouse; photograph, *c.* 1930 52
3.40 The Church of St Mary and St Nicholas, Littlemore; photograph, *c.* 1930 53
3.41 Newman's academic hood 53
4.1 Oxford and Cambridge Coach; engraving from 1830 60
4.2 Plan of the cottages at Littlemore attached to Newman's lease 60
4.3 The College 61
4.4 The College, view toward the library 61
4.5 and 4.6 "The Newman-Ooth College"; satirical print, original in St Mary's College, Oscott 62
4.7 Cottage No. 1, The College; painting by Dawn Hippwell, late 1970s 63
4.8 The College; painting by Lorraine Bewick, *c.* 2001 63
4.9 Breviary and photograph of John Dobrée Dalgairns 64
4.10 William Lockhart 64
4.11 Our Lady's Altar in the Passionist Monastery of S. Angelo di Vetralla 65
4.12 Bl. Dominic Barberi 65
4.13 The Angel Hotel, High Street, Oxford; engraving 66
4.14 Bl. Dominic Barberi; sketch by Dickie Doyle 66
4.15 Sculpture by Faith Tolkien, in the parish church of Bl. Dominic Barberi, Littlemore, 1995 67
4.16 The fireplace; painted by Br Seán McLaughlin, FSO, in 2006 67
4.17 Newman's writing desk in the College library 68
4.18 Relics of Blessed Dominic Barberi; on permanent loan from the Passionist Fathers 68

4.19 Exterior of the Church of St Ignatius, at St Clements; photograph by Bishop Dr Klaus Dick, 1993 69
4.20 Interior of the Church of St Ignatius; photograph *c.* 1910 69
4.21 – 4.24 Newman's private room at The College 70–71
4.25 Littlemore as depicted in the Newman window in Oriel College (design by Vivienne Haig, realisation by Douglas Hogg) 72
4.26 Oxford Observatory; engraving by G. Hollis 1836 73
4.27 Manuel Johnson; engraving of portrait by R.A. Richmond 73
4.28 John Henry Newman and Ambrose St John; painting by Maria Giberne in Birmingham Oratory, *c.* 1846–7 74
4.29 Chapel of Propaganda Fide, Rome 75
4.30 Alb in which Newman is supposed to have celebrated his first Mass 75
5.1 St Philip Neri celebrating Mass in the catacombs of St Sebastian; watercolour 83
5.2 St Philip's death mask 83
5. 3 Engraving of Old Oscott, Newman's 'Maryvale' 84
5.4 Our Lady of Victory in the chapel of Maryvale 84
5. 5 John Henry Newman in 1851; print of painting by Maria Giberne 85
5.6 The first Oratory in Alcester Street; after original drawing by John L. Baker 85
5. 7 John Henry Newman; engraving from *Whitehall Revue*, 10 May 1879 86
5. 8 Unfinished painting by Dickie Doyle of the first Synod of Westminster (1852); original in St Mary's College, Oscott 87
5.9 Chapel of St Mary's College, Oscott; engraving 87
5.10 Paul Cardinal Cullen 88
5.11 Newman House, Dublin, interior 88
5.12 Newman House, Dublin, exterior 88
5.13 The University Church, Dublin, entrance; photograph by Denis Riches 89
5.14 The University Church, Dublin, interior 89
5.15 Newman's teapot 90
5.16 Newman's shaving mirrors, boot hook, handkerchief, and pocket diary 90

5.17 – 5.18 John Henry Newman at the Oratory in Birmingham in 1861; photographs by Heath and Beau 91
5.19 John Henry Newman; photograph 92
5.20 John Henry Newman; *carte-de-visite* photograph by Heath and Beau 92
5.21 John Henry Newman; 19th century oil painting based on photograph by Mclean and Haes 93
5.22 The present Oratory School in Woodcote near Reading; pencil drawing 94
5.23 John Henry Newman; photograph by Heath and Beau, 1861 94
5.24 John Henry Newman; photograph 95
5.25 John Henry Newman; photograph by Mclean and Haes, 1864 95
5.26 Frederick William Faber; engraving 96
5.27 John Henry Newman's library in the Birmingham Oratory 96
5.28 John Henry Newman, 1864; photograph by R.W. Thrupp 97
5.29 John Henry Newman, *c.* 1870; photograph by R.W. Thrupp 97
5.30 John Henry Newman; *carte-de-visite* portrait 97
5.31 Newman's rosary 98
5.32 Henry Edward Cardinal Manning; *carte-de-visite* photograph by Pierre Petit 98
5.33 Sr Maria Pia (Maria Giberne); detail of watercolour self-portrait, after 1863 99
5.34 *Letter to Pusey*; title page 100
5.35 E. B. Pusey; engraving 100
5.36 John Henry Newman; plaster copy of the bust by Thomas Woolner 101
5.37 John Henry Newman, 1867; photograph 101
5.38 Letter of John Henry Newman to Revd G. W. Huntingford 102
5.39 John Henry Newman, 1868; postcard of painting by A.R. Venable, 1868, in Oxford Oratory 103
5.40 Ambrose St John; photograph 103
5.41 Henry Wilberforce; *carte-de-visite* 104
5.42 Samuel Wilberforce, Bishop of Oxford; *carte-de-visite* 104

5.43 John Henry Newman; engraving by Samuel Cousins after a drawing by Lady Coleridge 105
5.44 John Henry Newman; watercolour 106
5.45 John Henry Newman; photograph 107
5.46 John Henry Newman; engraving from *The Illustrated London News*, 17 May 1879 107
6.1 Cardinal Newman; photograph by unknown photographer in Rome 114
6.2 Photograph of cover of first edition of the Biglietto Speech 115
6.3 John Henry Newman; portrait by Emmeline Deane dated 6 September 1884 115
6.4–6.5 Newman's study at the Birmingham Oratory, 116
6.6 Cardinal Newman; after the painting by Ossiani 116
6.7 Newman with the Oratory Fathers 117
6.8 Cardinal Newman; engraving after the painting by Walter William Ouless (1878) 117
6.9 Cardinal Newman; photograph 118
6.10 Memorial print of the late Cardinal J.H. Newman, supplement to *The Illustrated London News*, 10 October 1890 118
6.11 Cardinal Newman; photograph 119
6.12 Cardinal Newman; photograph by H.J. Whitlock 119
6.13 Cardinal Newman; photograph by Barraud, *c.* 1888 120
6.14 Cardinal Newman reading; photograph 120
6.15 Memorial plaque of John and Jemima Mozley 121
6.16 Bust of Cardinal Newman, Trinity College Garden, Oxford; photograph by Elke Deimel 122
6.17 St Philip Neri Chapel in the Birmingham Oratory Church 123
6.18 Cardinal Newman; wax portrait, 1990 123
6.19 Cardinal Newman; photograph 124
6.20 Cardinal Newman's study at the Birmingham Oratory; photograph, *c.* 1958 124
6.21 Memorial statue of Cardinal Newman outside the London Oratory 125
6.22 Fr Henry Lewis Bellasis, CO, and Cardinal Newman; photograph 125
6.23 Cardinal Newman; three photographs 126

6.24 Cardinal Newman reading; after an oil painting 126
6.25 Cardinal Newman, *carte-de-visite* portrait 127
6.26 William Ullathorne; painting by Richard Burchett 128
6.27 Acceptance card to 1888 Birmingham music festival 129
6.28 Cardinal Newman's private chapel, Birmingham Oratory; photograph (14 July 1993) 130
6.29 Cardinal Newman's Titular Church, San Giorgio in Velabro, Rome 130
6.30 Cardinal Newman; posthumous painting by George Allen Warner, oil on slate 131
6.31 John Henry Cardinal Newman; painting by Emmeline Deane, 1889 132
6.32 – 6.33 Cardinal Newman, photographs from his last photograph sitting 133
6.34 Death certificate of John Henry Cardinal Newman 134
6.35 Memorial Card 134
6.36 Report after Newman's death, *The Times* 13 August 1890 135
6.37 Notice of Newman's death, *The Times* 12 August 1890 135
6.38 Gravestone of John Henry Cardinal Newman and Ambrose St John, Rednal; photograph by Elke Deimel 136

Abbreviations of Newman's Works

(Unless indicated with the place, publisher and date of publication, all works are of the uniform edition first published by Longmans, Green, and Co., London, 1868-81, and published more recently, though not in its entirety, by Christian Classics, Westminster, MD, 1966-73.)

Addresses	*Addresses to Cardinal Newman with his replies*
Apo.	*Apologia Pro Vita Sua*
AW	*Autobiographical Writings*
Campaign	*My Campaign in Ireland*
HS, I, II, III	*Historical Sketches*
Idea	*The Idea of a University*
LD	*The Letters and Diaries of John Henry Newman*
LG	*Loss and Gain*
MD	*Meditations and Devotions*
NO	*Newman the Oratorian: His Unpublished Oratorian Papers*
Phil.N., I, II	*The Philosophical Notebook of John Henry Newman*
Prepos	*Present Position of Catholics in England*
PS, I-VIII	*Parochial and Plain Sermons*
SVO	*Sermons Preached on Various Occasions*
VV	*Verses on Various Occasions*

Bibliography

I. John Henry Cardinal Newman

A. Bibliographical Sources, Indices, Lexica, etc.

Artz, J., *Newman-Lexikon*. Mainz: Matthias Grünewald Verlag, 1975.

Blehl, V. F., *John Henry Newman: A Bibliographical Catalogue of His Writings*. Charlottesville, Virginia: University Press of Virginia, 1978.

Earnest, J. D. and Tracey, G., *John Henry Newman: An Annotated Bibliography of His Tract and Pamphlet Collection*. New York and London: Garland Publishing, Inc., 1984.

Rickaby, J., S.J., *Index to the Works of John Henry Cardinal Newman*. London: Longmans, Green and Co., 1914.

B. Books

(Unless indicated with the place, publisher and date of publication, all works are of the uniform edition first published by Longmans, Green, and Co., London, 1868-81, and published more recently, though not in its entirety, by Christian Classics, Westminster, MD, 1966–73.)

Addresses to Cardinal Newman with his replies etc. 1879–81. Edited by the Rev. W. P. Neville, New York, London, and Bombay: Longmans, Green, and Co., 1905

Apologia Pro Vita Sua, ed. I. Ker, London: Penguin Books, 1994.

Autobiographical Writings, ed. Henry Tristram. London: Sheed & Ward, 1956.

Discourses on the Scope and Nature of University Education addressed to the Catholics of Dublin, Dublin: James Duffy, 1852

My Campaign in Ireland, Part I, Catholic University Reports and other Papers, printed for private circulation only by A. King & CO: Aberdeen, 1896

Historical Sketches

The Idea of a University

The Letters and Diaries of John Henry Newman, ed. Charles Stephen Dessain, et al., Vols. I-X (Oxford: Oxford University Press, 1978–2007), XI-XXII (London: Thomas Nelson and Sons Ltd,

1961–72), XXIII-XXXI (Oxford: Oxford University Press, 1973–77).
Loss and Gain
Meditations and Devotions
Newman Family Letters, Introduced and edited by Dorothea Mozley, SPCK, London 1962
Newman the Oratorian: His Unpublished Oratorian Papers, ed. Placid Murray OSB, Leominster: Gracewing, 1980
Parochial and Plain Sermons
The Philosophical Notebook of John Henry Newman. Edited by Edward J. Sillem, 2 Vols, Louvain: Nauwelaerts Publishing House, 1969 and 1970.
Present Position of Catholics in England, ed. Andrew Nash, Leominster: Gracewing, 2000
Parochial and Plain Sermons, 8 Vols.
Sermons Preached on Various Occasions, ed. James Tolhurst, Leominster: Gracewing, 2007
Verses on Various Occasions

II. Secondary Sources

Birmingham Cause of Canonization of the Servant of God John Henry Cardinal Newman (1801-1890). Founder of the English Oratories, Positio Super Virtutibus, published by V. F. Blehl, Rome, 1989
Ker I., *John Henry Newman*. A Biography, Oxford: Oxford University Press, 2009
Lockhart W., *Cardinal Newman. Reminiscences of Fifty Years Since,* London: Burns & Oates, 1891
Trevor M., *Light in Winter*, London: Macmillan, 1962
The Pillar of the Cloud, London: Macmillan, 1962
Ward W., *The Life of John Henry Cardinal Newman based on his private journals and correspondence,* 2 Vols., London, New York, Bombay and Calcutta: Longmans, Green & Co, 1912

Acknowledgements

The Spiritual Family The Work thanks everybody who has contributed to our specialized Newman Library and to our permanent exhibition on *Newman and his Times* at The College in Littlemore Oxford over the years. We regret that it was not possible to include all the exhibits in this book. We bear deepest gratitude to each and every one of you in our hearts, and we want to thank all our friends and benefactors whose generous support enables us to fulfil our mission at The College for the good of the Church.

We are very grateful to Mr. Michael Pitt-Payne, who patiently and with expertise photographed all the items of the exhibition.

We thank the staff of Family Publications and of Gracewing Publishing, who have helped to realise this project.